T0414116

DESIGNER'S NEXT

22 ARCHITECTS & INTERIOR DESIGNERS DEFINING TOMORROW

BETA-PLUS

In 2019, our book *GENERATION NEXT - ARCHITECTS & INTERIOR DESIGNERS DEFINING TOMORROW* was published, an absolute bestseller in our collection which has been reprinted three times in three years.

After four years, the successor, *DESIGNER'S NEXT,* is now being published, with a carefully curated selection of twenty-one promising architects, interior architects and designers.

As in the first edition, this is once again an eminently international group: individuals and duos from Belgium, the United Kingdom, France, the Netherlands, the United States, Spain, Australia, Ukraine and Canada.

They each show one or more of their recent private projects in an extensive report with portrait and biography.

We wish the reader much pleasure and inspiration with this book.

We can warmly recommend all these designers for guiding your own living or interior projects.

Wim Pauwels
Publisher

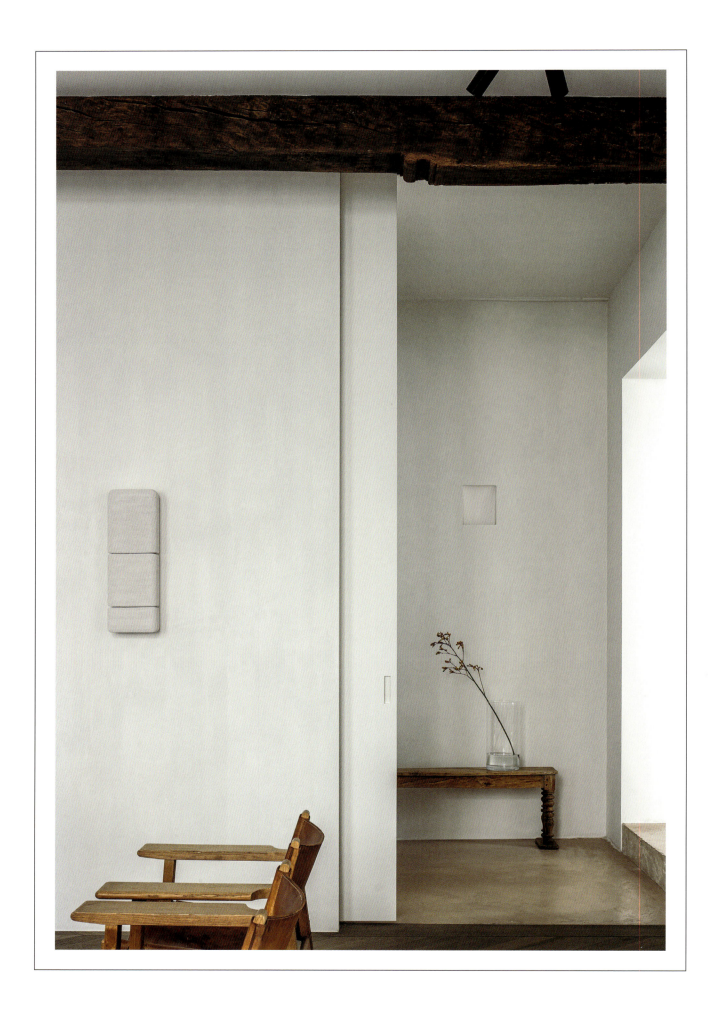

Contents

Britt Van Namen

Design studio Britt Van Namen stands for timeless interior designs and clean functionality that closely match the architecture of a project. The designs of Britt and her design team are characterized by their minimalist simplicity and subtle details.

"Your story shapes my design. Therefore, I always start from the client's desires, wishes and expectations. As an interior designer, I distill from that a design that reflects the essence of your vision."

Unity between light, form and space is the common thread in the designs of design studio Britt Van Namen. An eye for detail lifts an interior to a higher dimension and carefully selected materials create a timeless and contemporary look and feel.

Old Monastery Turnhout

This old monastery was converted into apartments, with the beautiful chapel as the absolute highlight. The classical elements of the original chapel were preserved - high ceilings, beautiful glass - and supplemented with contemporary architecture.

The first floor, for example, was glazed to emphasize the connection with the garden and to allow as much light as possible into the building. On the ground floor, the kitchen in particular attracts attention with its forward cabinets, in which all appliances are concealed. Two islands provide a cooking and rinsing function, with taps from Quooker in patina bronze. The tablets in illusion bronze-natural stone create a beautiful effect, and run into the cut-out cooking hobs. In the living space, a large custom-made wall unit with gas fireplace by Metalfire attracts attention. Recessed sliding doors hide the TV. The master suite is also on the ground floor, complete with original church windows and dressing room with sliding doors. The adjacent eggplant-colored bathroom has white and green accents and was finished with eucalyptus veneer, which is also found in the living space and dressing room. The pattern of the breccia capraia natural stone adds an additional eye-catcher to the bathroom and harmonizes beautifully with the Makro faucets in brushed steel. Placing the eggplant-colored bathtub with bronze technology in the bedroom created space in the bathroom for a double shower with bench seat, which continues into the washbasin. Two glass walls and a low organic piece of furniture in the adjacent dressing room create a spatial effect and connect the different rooms.

In this total renovation, organic forms in particular play a major role. These include the curved doorways, the rounded kitchen islands and the organic staircase in steel. And also the suspended ceiling in the master suite received an arch. Indirect lighting with hidden LED lines emphasize these shapes, while spotlights on the church windows provide colorful accents. The incoming natural light accentuates the painting techniques. The upstairs is set up as a TV room with a built-in bedroom cove.

This exceptional renovation by Britt Van Namen was requested by the renowned company Texture Painting, which has grown from a high-end painting company to a total provider of unique, decorative techniques.

Photography: Cafeine (Thomas De Bruyne)

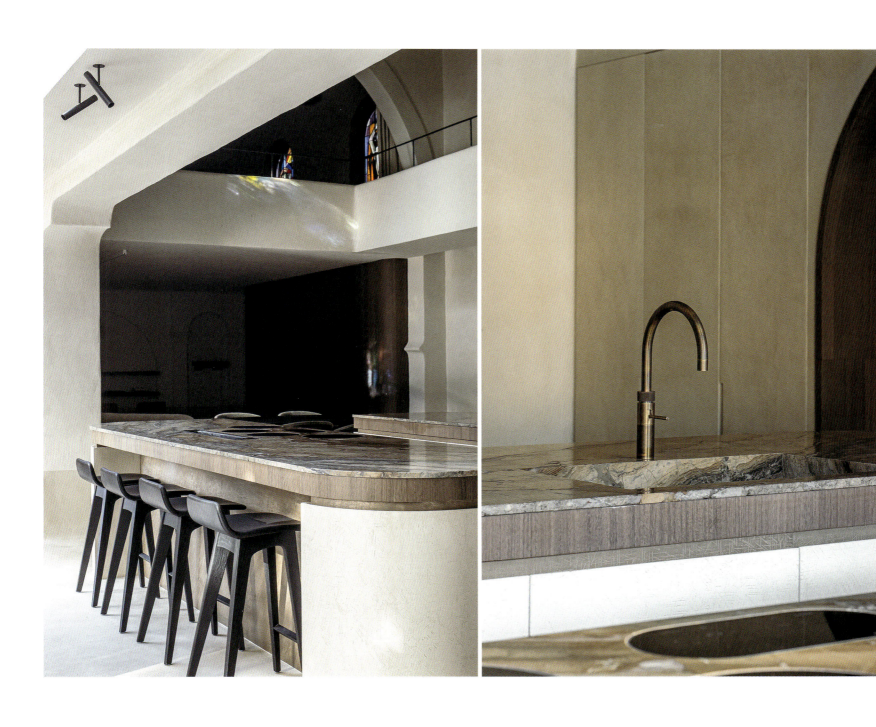

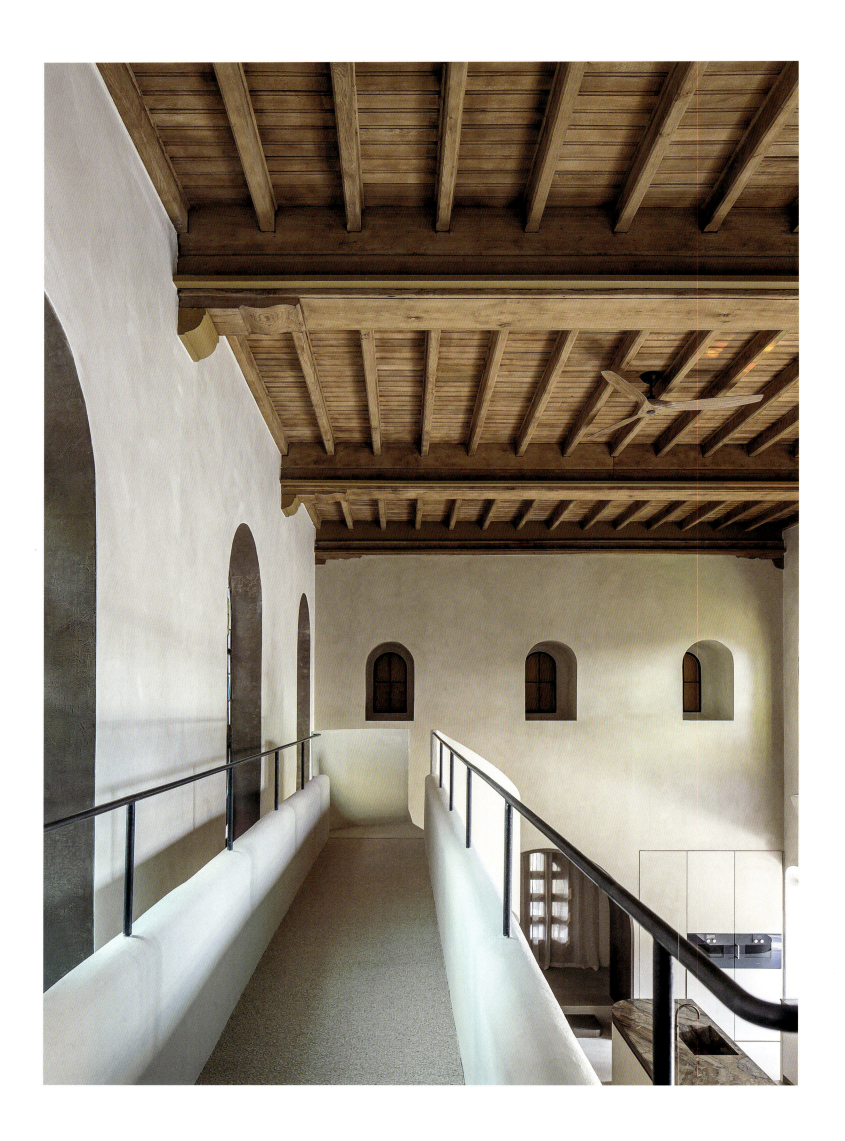

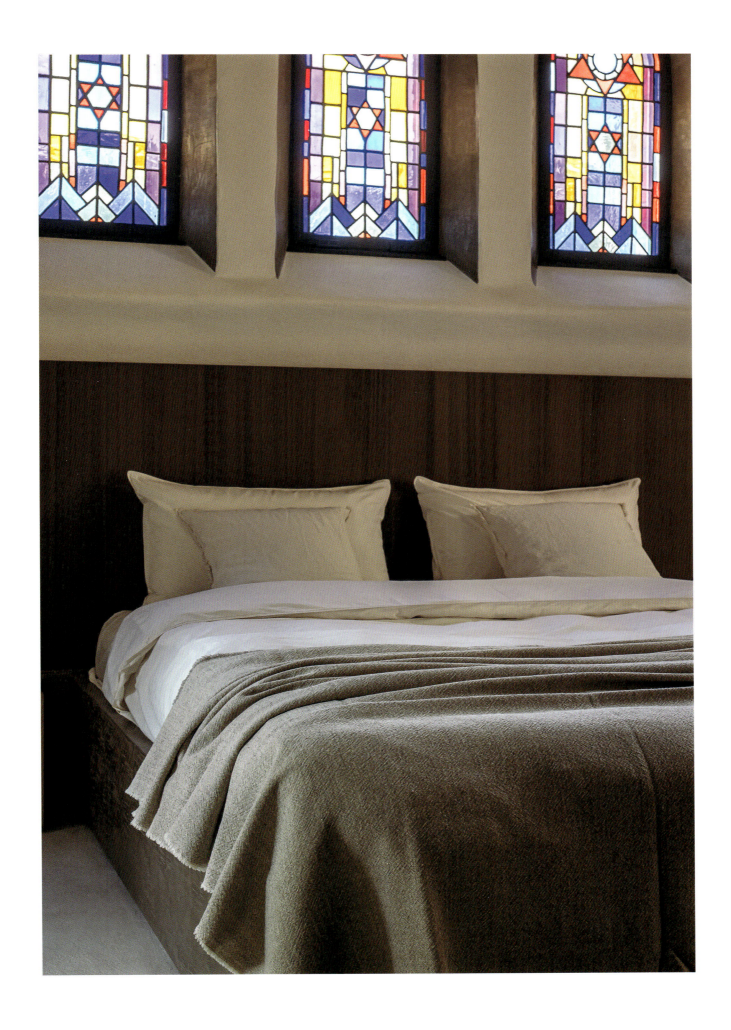

Louisa Grey

Over the past two decades, British interior design studio House of Grey have crafted a signature aesthetic which has gathered momentum across the global design community. As a pioneering design studio their fundamental aim has become the need to leave a positive design legacy when renovating and restoring modern and historic spaces, for both residential or commercial use.

Their purpose is to create interior landscapes that have inherent health benefits and minimal impact on the planet. They have developed a whole-person-whole-world approach to designing and building spaces for their clients which combines House of Grey's signature aesthetic with Salutogenic Design principles and cradle-to-cradle materials. They call this: Circular Salutogenic Design.

House of Grey consistently demonstrates across their Private Client and Hospitality portfolio of work that ecological building and sustainable design doesn't mean the owner or client needs to compromise on aesthetics. A building or a space can still be practical, durable, and ethical, as well as beautiful, comfortable and luxurious.

Each of our studio members are trained in the key skills for effective design and immersed in the House of Grey philosophy.

Founder and Creative Director Louisa Grey has 22 years experience in interior design and styling that spans designing luxury apartments for major developers, to private residential renovations. Louisa is renowned for her holistic approach to design in both work and life.

Home of Holism

Home of Holism gently challenges the concept of 'retreat'. Instead of looking far afield to find an escape from daily life, its creators - House of Grey - start the search a little closer to home. Home of Holism is an example of how one's day to day home and work environments can be restful and restorative, and provide the solace and serenity required to recharge and relax.

"Limiting stress starts with the environments we live and work in. If the home provides your daily retreat, there is no reason why the workplace cannot transcend to the same level." says Louisa Grey, Founder of House of Grey.

Behind Home of Holism's townhouse façade are interiors that invite one to live the 'holiday life'. The holistic approach taken to the design considers not just how items and materials look and feel, but also, how they perform for the seamless running of a home or workspace.

The materials used have been chosen in line with House of Grey's sustainability principles and for their Circular Salutogenic Design qualities. Non-toxic, natural resources are the focus, as they create calm, reduce stress and increase cognitive performance, boosting collective creativity.

Photography: Michael Sinclair

Jim Dierckx

Jim Dierckx is an interior architect with more than 10 years of experience in mainly residential renovations and interior design. His office is located in Antwerp but their projects are spread all over Belgium. Jim and his team focus mainly on high-end residential projects with an objective to restore the authenticity of the property.

Their work is characterized with warm pure materials embraced in a timeless design following classical principles. Great attention is paid to architectural lines, vistas, layout, and light play. An approach that encompasses all aspects with respect and deep understanding for the client's needs and wishes to ultimately create a harmonious whole between the identity of the builder and the property. Spatial functionality, simplicity and light and are the key components of their work.

www.jimdierckx.com

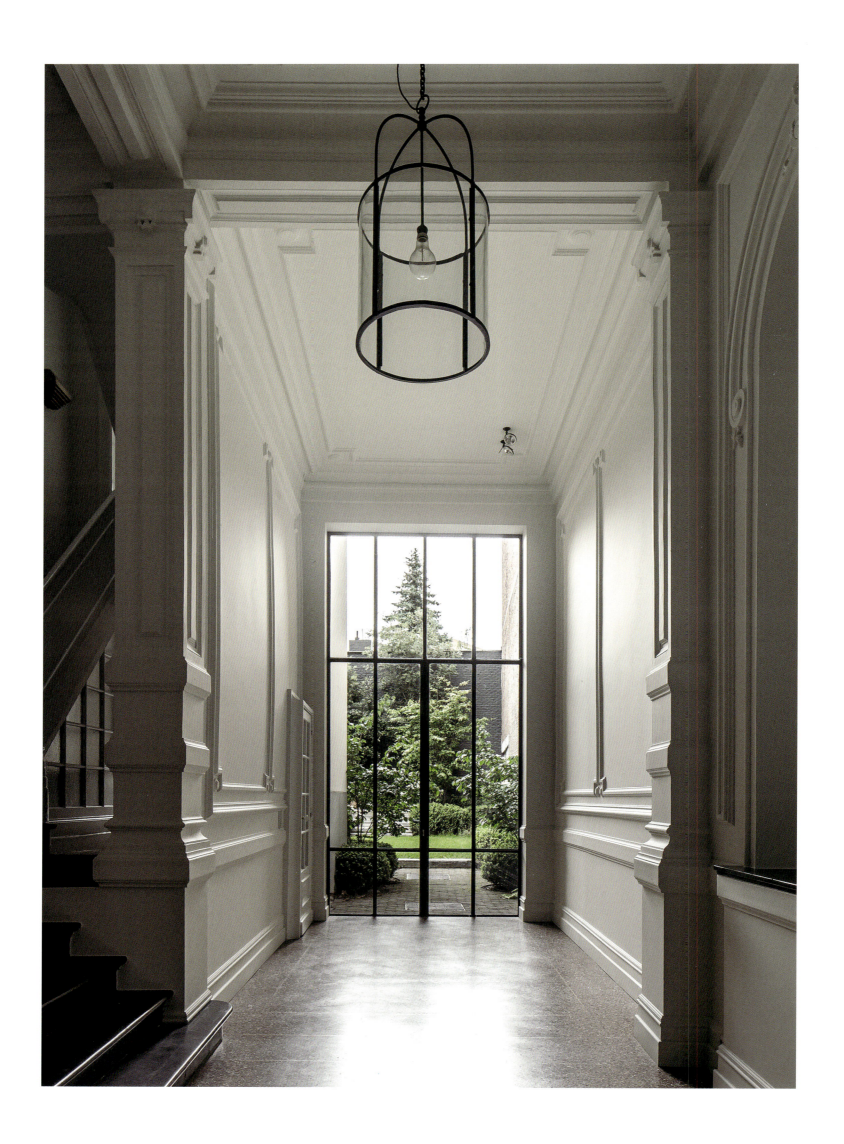

Two total renovations

On pages 36-43: This property is a majestic townhouse located in Antwerp. This was a total project by team Jim Dierckx; a renovation of the entire property to the total interior and garden design. Over the years and previous renovations, the property had lost much of its charm. With this project they wanted to extend the authenticity and class of the exterior facade to the interior of the house. To create a pleasant dynamic, the ground floor is connected to the second floor by a void. A large steel window on the rear facade connects both floors to draw in as much natural light as possible.

In the design and execution of the works, a balance was sought between authenticity and contemporary comfort. The design and proportions of the design follow classical principles. For finishing, moulures were restored and added. The floors are finished with terrazzo and marble, oak planks according to original laying pattern.

On pages 44-49: This spacious loft is located in the city center of Antwerp. This project is a total renovation up to and including furnishing. Jim Dierckx and his team have highlighted the limited original elements of the property as much as possible. The design and finishes employ a pared-down simplicity in keeping with classic principles. The house is u-shaped with the living spaces wrapping around the courtyard. The windows have been adapted to draw in as much natural light as possible.

For the finishes, only natural and pure materials were used; concrete, old oak, marble, steel and linen. The decor is a coherence of custom furniture designed in-house combined with modern & vintage design and antique trouvailles.

Photography: Cafeine (Thomas De Bruyne)

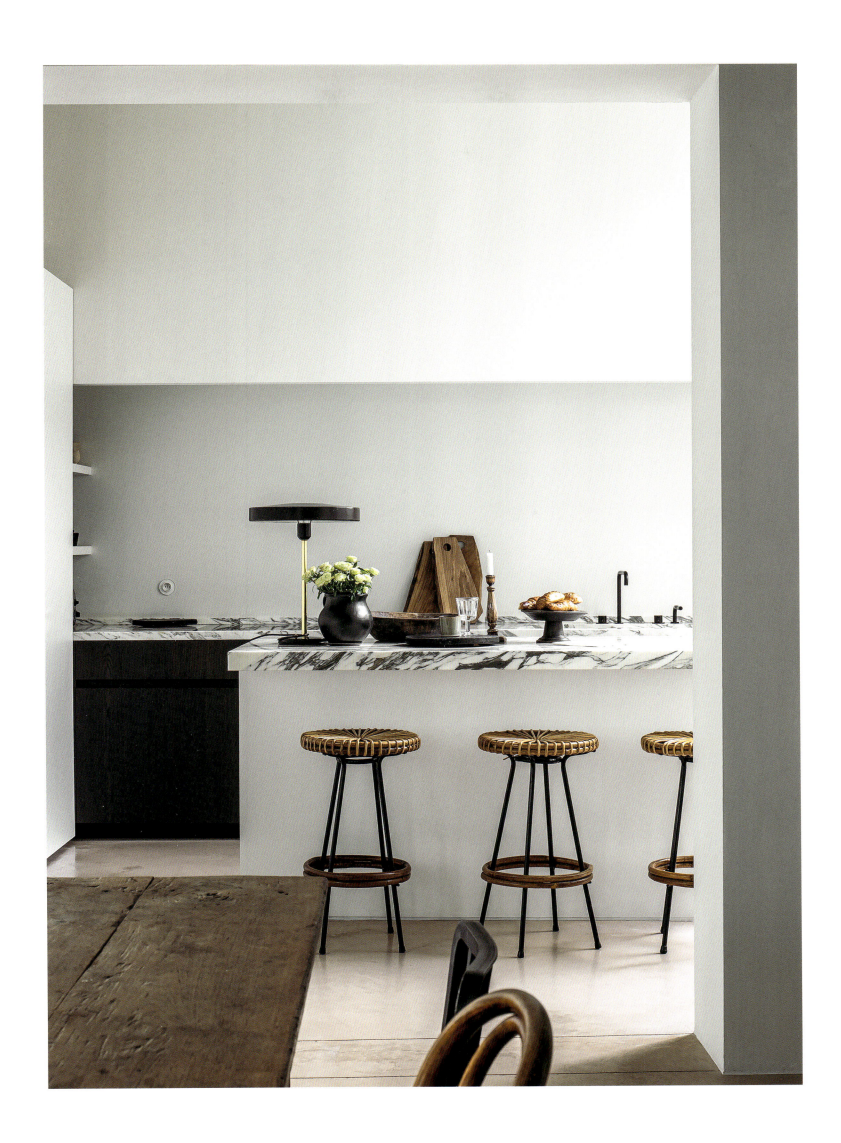

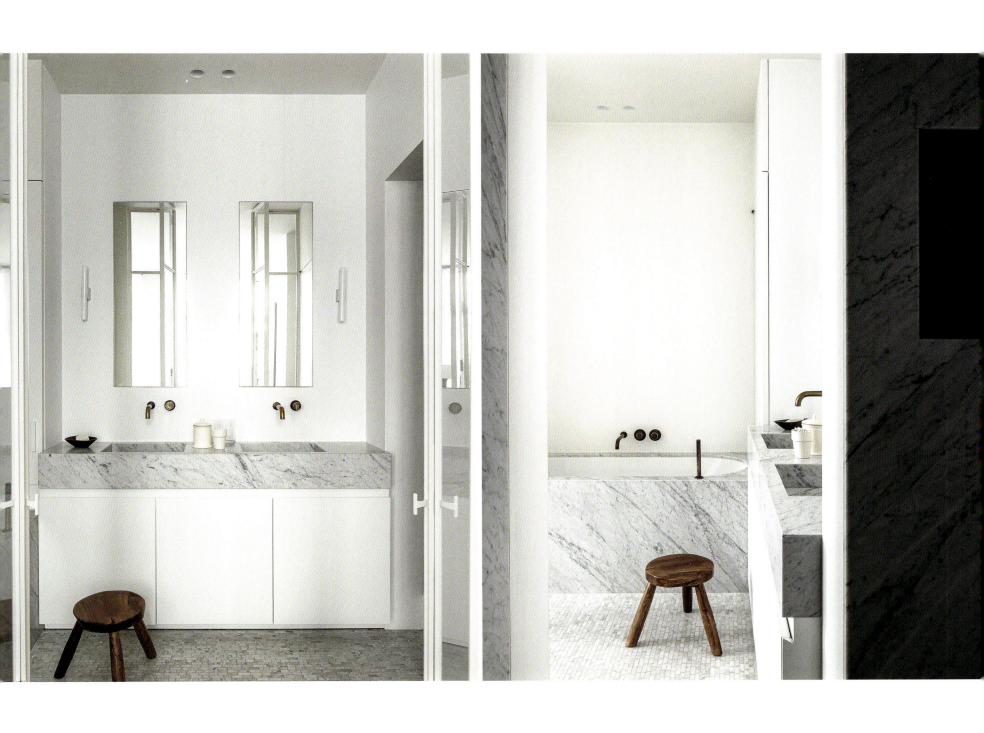

Jessica Berguig
and Francesco Balzano

AFTER BACH came about following the meeting of two confirmed aesthetes, passionate about decoration, materials and art: Jessica Berguig, owner of the JAG gallery, and Francesco Balzano, designer of high-quality, limited-edition objects and furniture for the design studio that bears his name.

Both built up their experience, Jessica over several years of her own interior design projects, and Francesco over eight years as Project Director with Joseph Dirand. Their apprenticeship was based on experimenting with high-quality raw materials, giving particular attention to the quality of detailing.

Francesco and Jessica design environments that are refined and welcoming, in which the furniture and art pieces resonate with the space. Gentle, quiet atmospheres that express the fruit of a collaborative design.

Working in tandem, their skill was first demonstrated in the new flagship concept for chocolate-maker DAMYEL in Paris. The project won the ADC Award 2020 for best shop in the interiors category.

In the wake of this, they created interior design studio AFTER BACH in December 2020.

www.afterbach.com

Avenue Montaigne, Paris

Montaigne is the first residential project by the After Bach studio.

Located on Paris' prestigious Avenue Montaigne, this two-floor apartment has been redesigned as a sophisticated, modern haven.

Francesco Balzano and Jessica Berguig drew their inspiration from David Lynch's film Mulholland Drive. The space has been designed like a 1950s American house, with walls panelled in French oak and natural plant fibre textiles.

The focal point of the main bathroom is a bathtub sculpted from a block of fine beige stone. A clever play of light has been created by means of louvered screens in natural oak.

The project's clean, precise lines dialogue with furniture by Jacques Adnet or George Nakashima, ceramics by Floris Wubben, and numerous pieces by contemporary artists and designers.

Arranged over two levels, the apartment benefits from a spectacular terrace overlooking Paris, and views of the Eiffel Tower.

Photography: Annick Vernimmen

Gregory De Bruyne and Elise Engelen

Oystr Studio offers an end-to-end interior design service, from concept to execution. All projects are fully bespoke, starting from scratch with mood boards and ideas that will evolve into a personal design with an eye for timeless quality and refinement.

Their portfolio consists of residential projects, offices and retail spaces as well as bespoke furniture design. All concepts are created in close dialogue with their clients, translating into the perfect balance between a functional and aesthetic space surrounded with subtle elements of surprise. Both sharing a love for warm materials and textures, there is a conscious balance between the various materials present in their designs.

Oystr Studio was founded by Elise Engelen and Gregory De Bruyne in 2020. Both obtained a Master's Degree in Interior Design at the University of Antwerp. The Studio is based in Antwerp, available worldwide.

Townhouse Project

For The Townhouse project, Oystr Studio was commissioned to create a city family home that merged both Parisian elegance and Japanese zen.

The house has been completely renovated with great respect for the original elements. The interior results in an aesthetic translation of the personality of the new residents, as well as their functional way of living as a family.

Every room was given an individual identity, playing with subtle colors, textures and light all coming together as in a balanced entity.

Photography: Ian Hermans

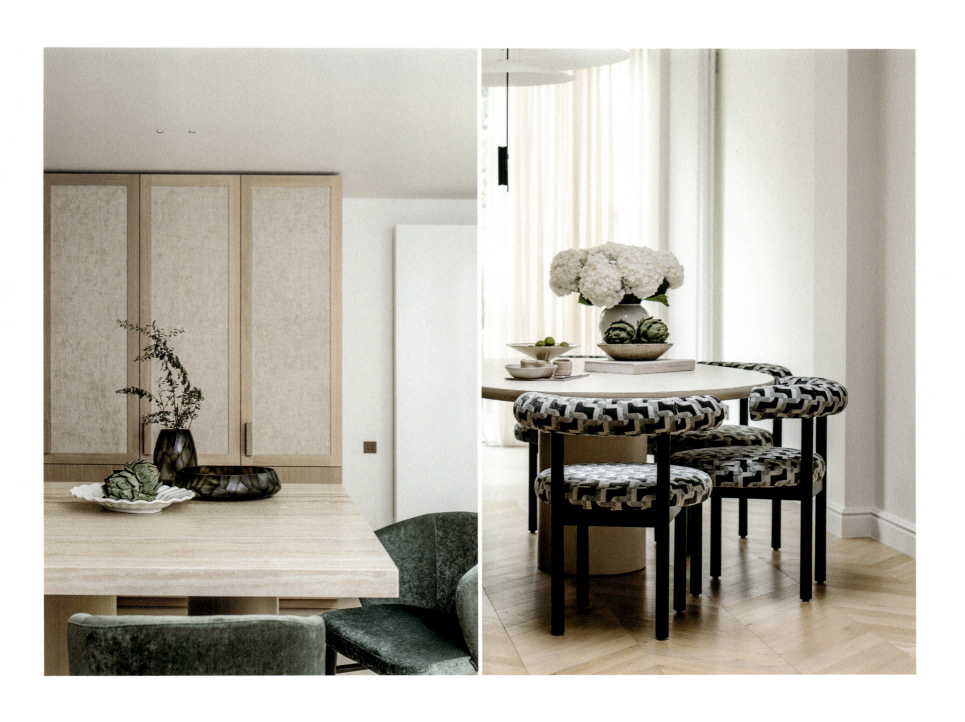

Anne Claus

With an eye for detail and an unerring sense of styling, Anne Claus designs interiors that are recognizable by their dedication and individuality.

Passion for various periods and styles make her interiors exciting, not bound by trends and therefore timeless.

Her love for art, materials and textures work their way into her interiors and lead to unexpected combinations, ultimately forming a whole where everything falls together.

www.anneclausinteriors.com

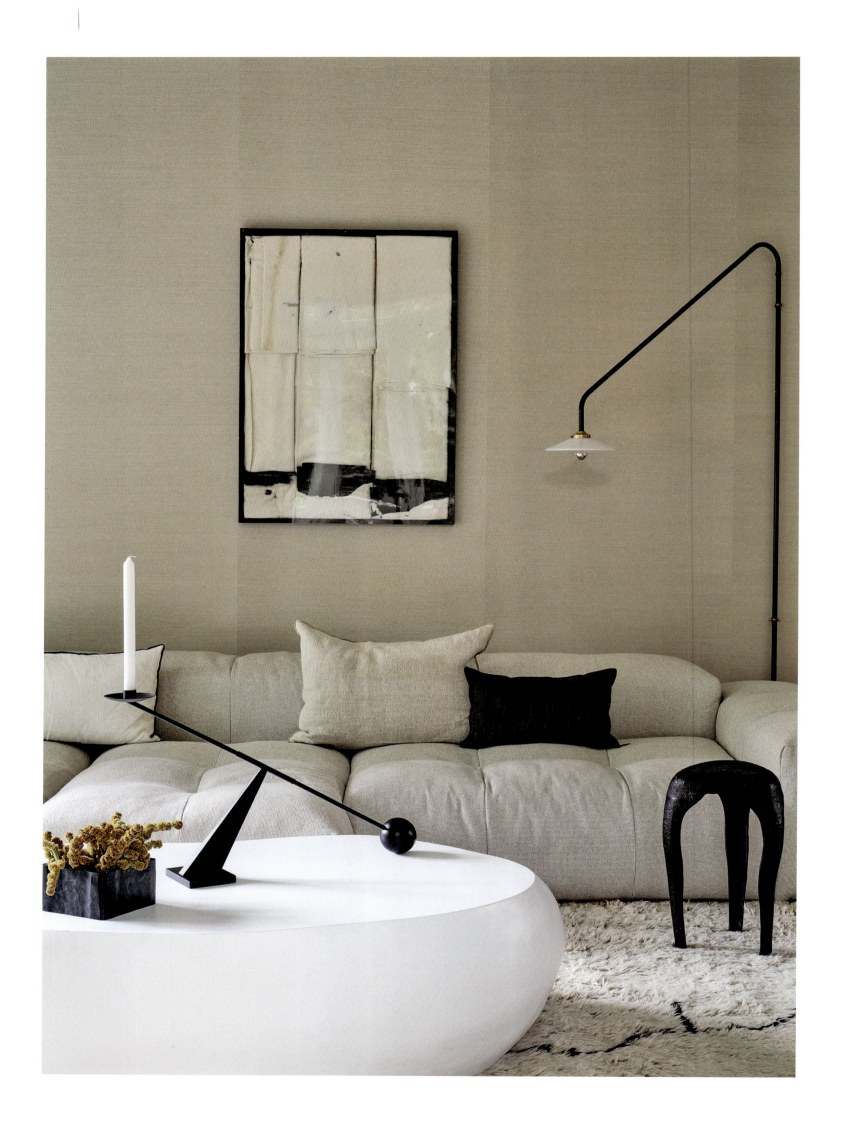

Residence in Hilversum

Anne Claus Interiors designed a modern interior in the Dutch city of Hilversum, with respect for the historical elements of the house.

This residence was designed for a young Amsterdam couple with children who were looking for more space. The house was in a rather bad condition, but thanks to its sublime classic details, such as ceiling mouldings, architraves, and panelling, the family was immediately attracted to the house. Both they and the interior studio wanted to maintain these elements. That meant much time of the renovation process went into scraping, restoring, and touching up those details. Some adjustments were made to the layout of the house. For instance, some walls were broken open, especially in the kitchen, creating a more open feeling. The client wanted a kitchen island, while the interior designer was convinced that the space should also have a dining table with bench seating. Thanks to a lot of puzzling, both wishes were met. An interesting detail is the meter cupboard, which could not be moved and was therefore concealed in the wooden column.

The other spaces needed much construction work as well. The bathrooms were connected to the bedrooms, doors were replaced, and cabinets were built in. Despite all this, you do not notice that there has been so much remodelling; on the contrary, the house gives the impression of having always had this layout. Finally, the floors were renewed as well. The woodwork in the residence was given a lighter colour, making the house a lot fresher. Furniture was chosen within the same neutral, calm colour spectrum. That way, they blended beautifully with the architectural details of the house and really let them shine.

The great strength of this residence is that the extensive renovation work effortlessly gives it a contemporary look, yet it does not forget its history. The combination of older elements with a soft colour palette creates a unique result that will provide quiet enjoyment for a long time to come.

Photography: Space Content Studio

Sebastian Zuchowicki

Sebastian Zuchowicki is an Argentine-American interior designer based in New York.

He studied at the New York School of Interior Design. Upon the start of his career, Zuchowicki worked with Studio Mellone and Studio Sofield prior to establishing his firm in 2020.

The studio primarily focuses on residential projects.

Sebastian Zuchowicki is a visual storyteller who transcends space through the use of fine art, objects and timeless interiors.

www.sebastianzuchowicki.com

Chelsea Project

Over the course of the year-long transformation of this 3,000-square-foot (280 square meter) home, Zuchowicki sought to append a traditional aesthetic to the modern architectural design of a renowned High Line building. The starting point was the living space, which Zuchowicki tends to begin his projects with, especially in New York City homes.

Zuchowicki adopted the philosophy of French Deco with a downtown twist, which he sought to achieve through layering textures and materials, and sourcing vintage and contemporary pieces.

From suede and velvet to linen and Venetian plaster, Zuchowicki found equilibrium in layering the various walls and doors of the space. Similarly, there was an opportunity to utilize the warmth of vintage pieces, such as Jacques Adnet sconces and a Jean Prouve sitting chair. On the other hand, a walnut ping-pong table was introduced as the dining table in order to add a playful, yet practical note.

One by one, Zuchowicki conceptualized each room, until the bedrooms, dining room and library were woven together with the living space, culminating in a subtle and timeless unity of the modern and traditional.

Photography: William Jess Laird

Angela Bermudez

Spanish architect and interior designer Angela Bermudez believes that, in some way, designing spaces is creating the scenography of our daily life. Creativity and imagination have constantly been core elements in her life as she has always had the desire to personalize and adapt her environment to her own needs.

There is nothing more beautiful than making your passion your profession, and that is why every step she has taken has led her to work in what she loves the most: designing and creating spaces.

After studying architecture at the ETSAM in Madrid and working for a year in a studio in Berlin, Angela continued working and expanding her knowledge about furniture, textiles, lighting ... in short, the tangible and livable, the 1:1 scale design.

Angela Bermudez gives great importance to the design of a good «box» as the main element for relaxed houses and fluid spaces, where beauty and harmony always go hand in hand with functionality. She seeks to create balanced and timeless environments, with a warm and cozy base using noble materials, a careful lighting and a good combination of fabrics, textures, and colors.

When working in a project, she considers it essential to communicate closely with the client to understand their tastes and needs. Each project should be understood as a special process and it should be adapted to each client in which the result is as important as enjoying the progress from end to end.

www.angelabermudez.com

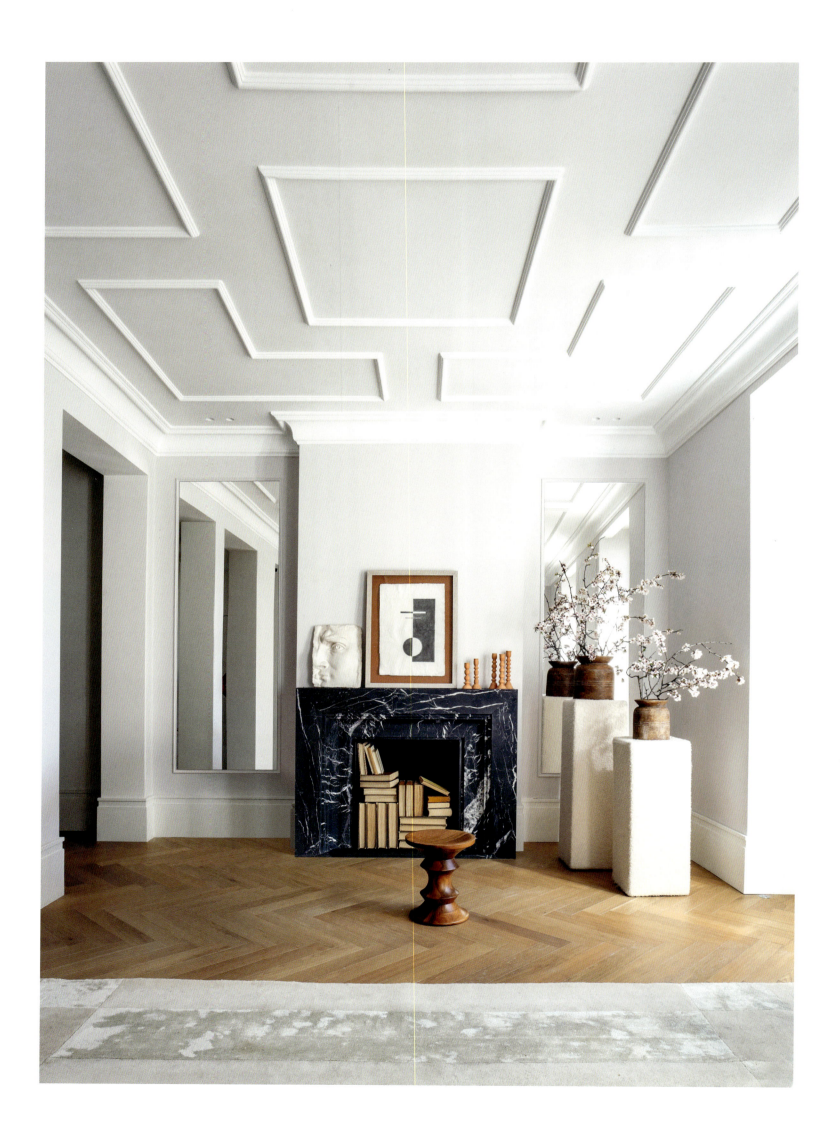

Mejia Lequerica, Madrid

Located in the historic Justicia district in Madrid, Angela Bermudez fully renovated and transformed this apartment from an old, dark and very divided house into a very bright and open space. The house distribution was adapted to the needs of the new owners but without losing the classic soul and essence of the early XXth century building.

The new layout eliminated hallways and connected the living room, dining room and kitchen creating an integrated public space in which to enjoy life with family and friends.

Given the intrinsic characteristics of the house, one of the key objectives of the project was to enhance the high ceilings using perimeter plaster molding and geometric motives. Moreover, the new design takes advantage of the light and the incredible views that come into the house through the classic wooden balconies.

It was sought to design a neutral base combining light tones in ceilings and walls and a herringbone oak parquet floor. On top of it, the combination of noble materials, such as black Nero Marquina marble or natural cherry wood, act as a common thread throughout the length and breadth of the house.

The decoration was carefully taken care by selecting special curated pieces and some custom made furniture, combining modern and classic elements which ultimately provide personality, sophistication and a timeless scenery.

Photography: Jaime Ferrer / Styling: Cristina Rodriguez Goitia

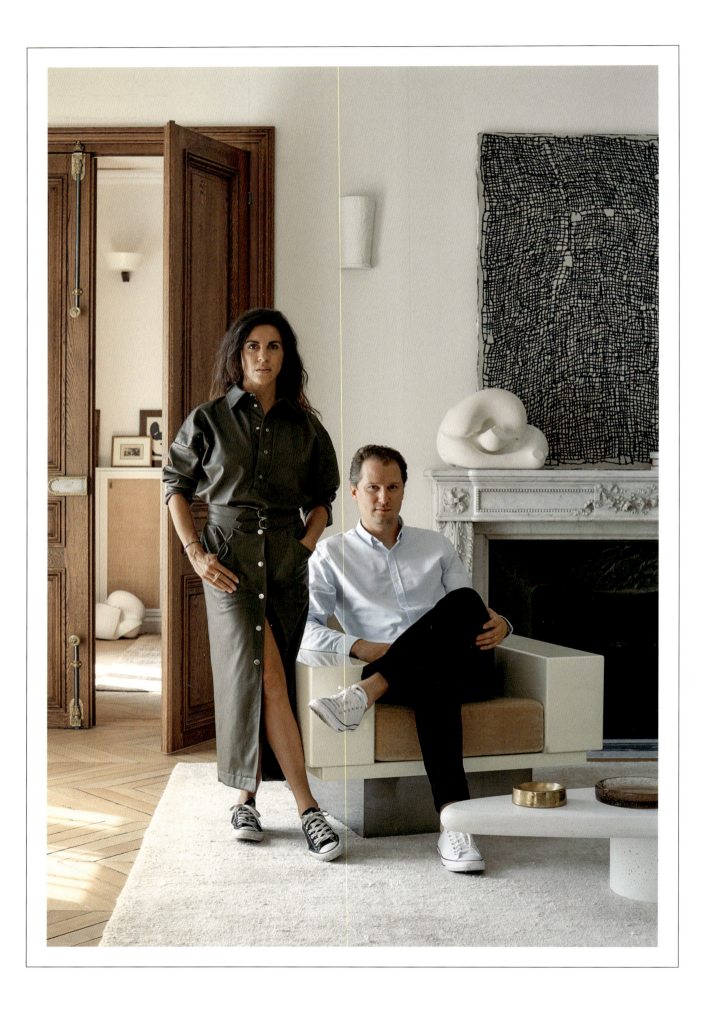

Stéphanie Lizée
and Raphael Hugot

After several years of collaboration in different Parisian agencies, Stéphanie Lizée and Raphael Hugot created in 2020 their own architecture studio Lizée-Hugot.

This association born from their complementarity allows them to express their narrative vision of interior architecture through accurate and sensitive places. The duo assumes its duality and makes it its strength. While Raphael Hugot affirms his affinity for the conception of plans and the balance of volumes, Stéphanie Lizée is fervently fond of the search for materials and know-how, the selection of unique pieces, the design of custom-made furniture and the mastery of decorative contrasts.

These roles allow them to affirm in the exchange a writing both singular and rigorous, to imagine functional places without superfluous, punctuated with daring and unexpected touches, full of emotions.

The Lizée-Hugot studio strives to give a soul to places without imposing or prescribing anything; the place deliberately left to accidents make the strength and authenticity of their achievements.

www.lizeehugot.com

Rue des Invalides Apartment

The owners of this quintessentially Parisian apartment overlooking Invalides asked interior designers Stéphanie Lizée and Raphaël Hugot to gently transform their 200 m² gem into a chic family home in the heart of Paris.

The new kitchen takes center stage in the apartment, and an elegant play of arches bathes the lounge and dining room in a sea of light. Everything here is sophisticated and discreet: the boiseries, the stucco, the patinated natural stone floor with cabochons, the bronze Art Déco handles, ... and with a light cloudscape by artist Nicolas Duyckaerts in the salon, to obscure the intrusive original ceiling painting.

Along with some striking recent projects (néo-diner Abstinence and the Hôtel des Académies et des Arts in Paris and Hôtel Le Sud in Juan-les-Pins, The Socialite Family's showroom, ...), this is yet another one of the promising duo's achievements finished to perfection.

Photography: Christophe Coënon

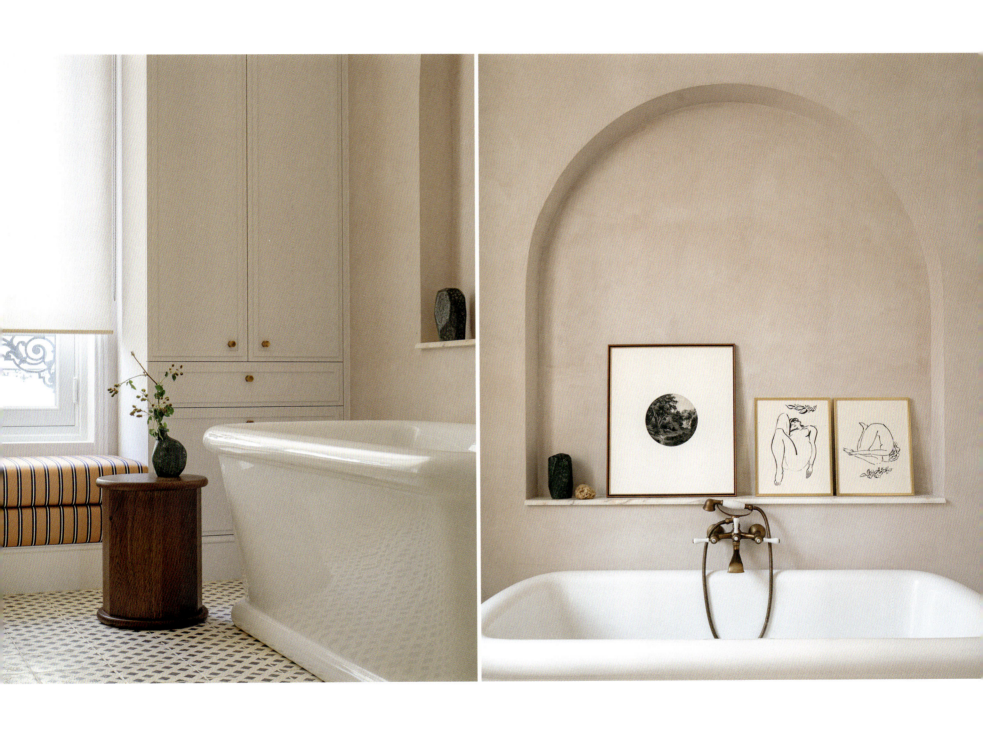

Thaïs Niville

Ville Design, created by interior designer Thaïs Niville, stands for quality with a eye for detail in sleekness, elegance and understated luxury in a contemporary and function design.

With a passion for space, light and lines, Thaïs Niville takes you into a creative world that fits your vision and budget.

Thaïs' interiors can best be described as timeless and neutral - "less is more".

Ville Design wants to assist clients in every phase of the design process with their knowledge and enthusiasm and they hope that even after all these years they are still satisfied with the choices made in consultation with them.

Their focus is that designs are tailor-made for the client and not based on trends. The goal is to find for each family the perfect organization of their home so that it becomes a place of home. In this way Thaïs and her team want to demonstrate the great added value of the studio.

The choice for sustainable and timeless materials takes every assignment to new insights and the challenge of an ever higher level.

Renovation and new construction projects at home and abroad form the basis for a creative portfolio tailored to the client.

www.villedesign.be

Residence PV

For Residence PV, a renovation of an old farmstead in Dworp, Flemish Brabant. The client pretty much gave carte blanche to Ville Design for the entire project. That yielded a beautiful result that completely matches Thaïs' studio.

The result ended up looking more like a newly built home rather than a renovation, which points to the strength and insight of the interior design studio.

Initially, their brief was to focus on the master suite and living space. Throughout the design, however, Thaïs and her team were given the opportunity to extend their style throughout the home. It was an opportunity they grabbed with both hands.

The client's main requirement was that the interior design of the home match the concept and natural stone of the kitchen, which were already established.

Furthermore, they were given complete freedom to translate Ville Design's vision into reality, right down to the smallest details. The white spiral staircase integrated by the architect at the client's request is a work of art in itself and an added value to this project.

The interior pieces are also just an added value to this project and make sure that all the details are right when you walk into the house. The Out of Line table by Bieke Casteleyn to the staircase is a beautiful centerpiece. The natural stone in the bathroom also speaks for itself and gives a luxurious feel to the master suite without being too much.

After all, Thaïs and her team always maintain the "less is more" motto.

Photography: Cafeine (Thomas De Bruyne)

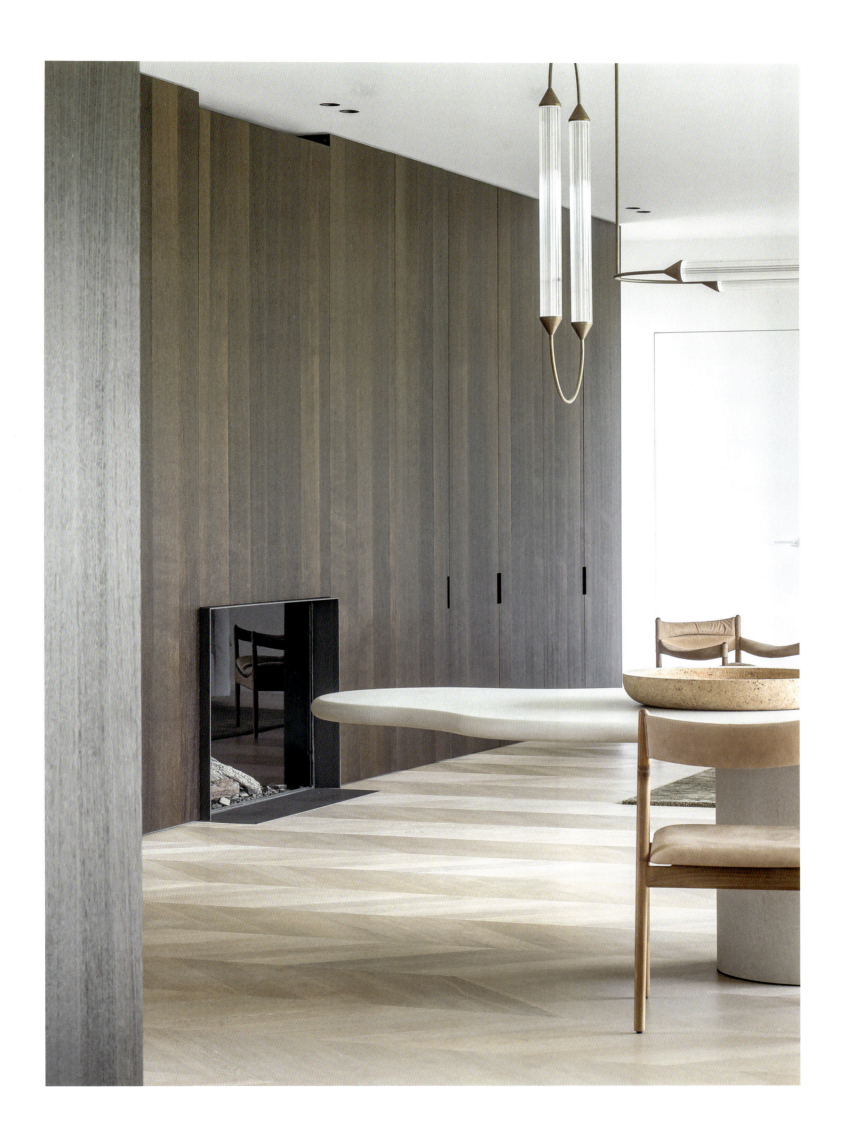

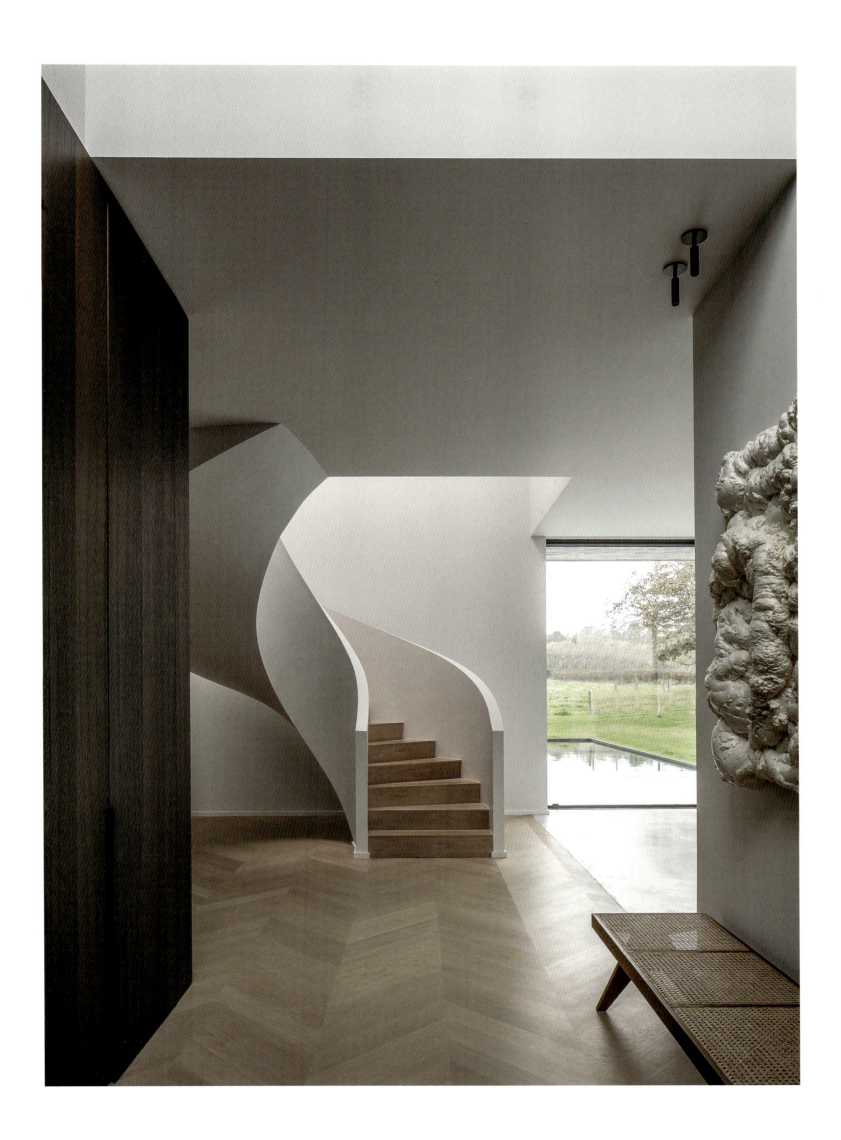

Nina Maya

Nina Maya Interiors specializes in beautiful bespoke residential and commercial interiors... "Purity of materials, unexpected elements, and custom designed details are the hallmarks of our style..."

Known for its tailored, polished spaces and precise, considered approach, Nina Maya Interiors has built a reputation for its unique customization of interiors to suit each individual project and client.

The studio based practice employs a dedicated team of architects, draftsman, designers & project managers all working collaboratively with artisans and master craftsman to provide an unparalleled level of beginning to end services to their clients both locally & Internationally.

Nina's passion for interior design and for creating meticulously curated, layered spaces is at the core of her practice and she leads her team with extensive design expertise, a career spanning a decade and a portfolio of highly refined projects.

www.ninamayainteriors.com

Pavillon House, Avalon (Sydney)

When Nina Maya and her husband bought a simple single-story house in Avalon, Sydney, it provided a blank canvas to create a dream design for a beach house, with every element custom designed, commissioned and crafted. Calm and idyllic, the luxury home showcases Nina Maya Interiors's approach and ethos, as well as the exceptional skill of the suppliers, artists and designers the studio works with.

The foundation of the Pavilion House is a four-bedroom pavilion home built in the 1980s. The previous owners had updated and extended the house about 10 years ago, but very little had been done to the original build otherwise, which was part of the attraction. It was literally a black box, and it represented the perfect blank slate. The house sits on a block of nearly 1,000 square metres, with the kitchen, dining and living area facing north to the pool, deck and garden. The four bedrooms are along the south side of the house, with two bathrooms (one of them newly integrated) in the middle of the floor plan. Large skylights illuminate these bathrooms.

The interiors truly exemplify Nina's design philosophy: "I like interior architecture and materiality to be minimal, clean, sleek and neutral. And because this is a beach house, we wanted to give it a retreat feel and for all the materials to be harmonious." The wall and ceilings in every room, and the floor of the living room, have a beautiful micro-cement coating that offers a velvety-textured neutral base. It has a subtle shimmer when it catches the light, especially on the wall beneath the six skylights along the edge of the living room. Kitchen joinery, including the range hood, is also coated with micro-cement so that it seamlessly blends into the walls, and the full-height joinery eliminates any superfluous lines. It also provides a minimalist backdrop to the Brescia green marble kitchen island and benchtops, which have been crafted in Italy.

Nina custom designed or commissioned all the furniture, lighting and artworks specifically for the house, including rugs and mirrors. The studio often designs one-off pieces for clients, and Nina saw the Pavilion House as an opportunity to expand the breadth of the collection. The lighting is also crafted exclusively for the house by Canadian lighting designer Randy Zieber. His kitchen pendant and master bedroom wall sconces are all made with alabaster, marble and bronze.

The artworks displayed throughout are all unique pieces, including the mesmerising Infinity Works light by artist Max Patté in the dining room and the playful resin form that local artist Tan Arlidge developed for the kitchen. Marisa Purcell designed the canvas piece that hangs in the lounge room, and a series of graphic works by Marcus Piper in collaboration with Axolotl are in all the bedrooms.

The block itself provided plenty of opportunity to develop the outdoors into different spaces for the family to use. A new pavilion to the side of the house contains an outdoor bathroom with sheer curtains that open to the pool. There is a new outdoor dining area at the top of the site, a circular fire pit, and huge gum trees, palm trees and expansive lawn. The result is a garden sanctuary that feels like a natural extension of the interior design; a place to enjoy the coastal landscape and climate in luxury and amenity.

The Pavilion House complements Nina's previous project, The Glasshouse in Paddington. Together, they represent the best of both worlds - coastal and city living at their finest - and showcase the adept eye and skill of the studio: two very different homes that are grounded in custom design, exceptional craftsmanship and offer luxury bespoke living.

Photography: Felix Forrest & Prue Roscoe

Rina Lovko

Rina Lovko is an architect and designer with more than a decade of working experience and a mastermind behind her eponymous Kyiv-based studio. Rina Lovko Studio, founded in 2008, specializes in private and public spaces. They have a lot of experience in working with private houses, apartments and commercial projects (showrooms, a beauty salon, a wine bar, a dental clinic, offices, a flower shop and a hairdresser).

Rina Lovko believes - each person and place dictate the conditions, and the architect, as a medium must be able to read them.

Only such an approach will give the desired result. All of this helps Rina Lovko Studio to create a unique world, where an architect and a client are sharing love to aesthetics and harmony.

www.rinalovko.com

Semerey - An apartment in Kyiv

The apartment is located on the 4th floor of a residential house, which was built in 1905, in the historical area of Kyiv. The space itself is luminous: all the windows overlook a quiet green park, and the light freely streams through them. Because of the state of the building, a massive renovation of the flat was required. The process of dismantling revealed the rotten slabs and large cracks in the walls, and that flooring replacement is needed.

Rina Lovko's client is a young woman, a fashion insider with a strong vision. This project is all about aesthetics, so it was entirely designed to meet her requirements and standards of beauty. The client is fascinated with Paris, so Rina's target was to recreate a flair of a vintage apartment. Her solution was not to copy the "Parisian chic" tricks, avoiding the ornamental plaster and other obvious elements of direct quotation of this style. The focus was shifted to natural textures, a combination of softness and determined details, and an overall airiness, and nuanced sophistication instead.

The state of the structure of the building made Rina renovate the apartment, and enhance the slabs and the walls. The old wooden inner walls were damaged by humidity and wood pests, so they had to remove them completely. The original parquet was also disassembled, and the floor was upgraded with a welded structure poured with concrete. Furthermore, Rina Lovko enhanced the balcony, and the walls were strengthened with special ties to pull together the frame.

Rina and her team opted for the time-tested scheme of the space arrangement, which is an enfilade. Given that the apartment is one-sided, they decided to design a long and functional hallway, containing an entrance wardrobe, a guest restroom, and a laundry area.

The kitchen is located near the living room entrance, and a cabinet with a refrigerator and an oven is a stand-alone element of this space. They managed to eschew the standardized modern solutions for the kitchen area when all the elements are built-in wall units. The bedroom can be seen through the double door from the living room, and the bedroom and the bathroom are separated with a glass partition. There is always a private zone at the end of an enfilade, and this time the bathroom fulfills this role. Consequently, the whole living area turned out to be bright and roomy, and the enfilade principle makes one area open to another, creating a coherent space. The airiness visually extends the apartment.

The walls were painted on top of plaster, with the deep texture being left as it is. The angle between walls and ceiling was smoothed out - this was a popular solution for the old flats in Kyiv.

Photography: Yevhenii Avramenko

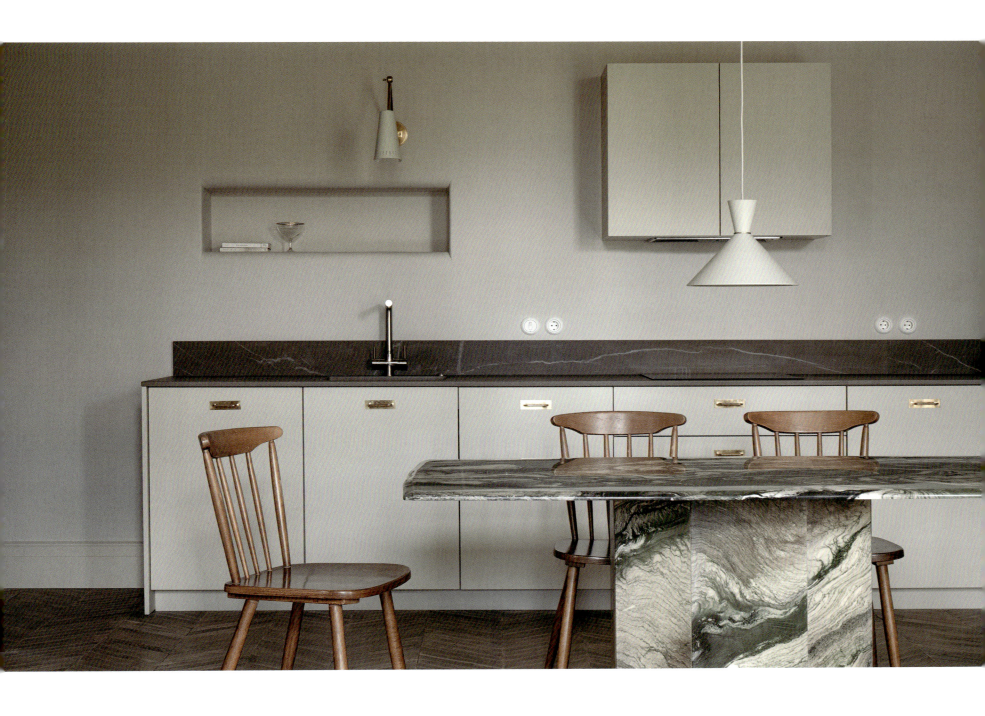

Sandra Weingort

Sandra Weingort is an internationally recognized and published interior designer. Born in Colombia, and residing between Miami and New York City, her style is the perfect blend of curated modern elegance and highly functional, timeless design.

A graduate of Parsons School of Design, Sandra honed her craft while working for the iconic William Sofeld of Studio Sofeld, where she served as design lead for a variety of high-end residential and retail projects. During this influential period, she learned to appreciate the critical relationship between designers and highly skilled craftsmen and decorative artisans.

Each project is unique, taking primary cues from a confluence of architectural context, the client and the desire to create a level of sophistication that is never pretentious.

Sandra's philosophy is that excellent design can only be achieved once it inspires a sense of levity and total ease, serving as an uplifting backdrop to one's daily life, never upstaging or overwhelming the lives or personalities of the inhabitants.

Poise and ease are achieved by balancing an artful sense of color and texture, highly bespoke custom furniture with impeccable attention to detail, and incorporating signifcant vintage and contemporary collectible design pieces that offer curiosity and a sense of wonder.

Sandra finds a commonality in her clients who share a healthy sense of humor and the wisdom that life is best lived when there is passion for its beauty and the joys it may bring.

www.sandraweingort.com

Vestry Street Apartment

After purchasing an apartment in Tribeca's upscale 70 Vestry, a striking complex designed by Robert A.M. Stern Architects, with interior architecture by Daniel Romualdez that overlooks the Hudson River, a couple with two children sought out interior designer Sandra Weingort.

The 3,000-foot (280 square meter) apartment may have been finalized with the building in 2018, but as one of the model units, it had been decorated with many additional flourishes and heavy finishes that were not originally specified by Romualdez. Sandra wanted to bring the interiors back to their original, simpler and more pure state, taking away a lot of the heavy and bold wall coverings, decorative finishes and random 'feature walls', so that the beautiful original architectural elements could shine through, and the art and furniture collection could be the central focus.

Comprised of three bedrooms, an office, enclosed kitchen/breakfast room and a living/dining area, the owners sought to create spaces that could be multifunctional. The living/dining room was meant to be a versatile space that felt sophisticated but discreet when hosting, and could also function as a relaxed family/media room, with a very comfortable and inviting feeling to gather intimately with themselves and their guests.

Sensing that the newly purchased apartment's décor was competing with her client's taste in art and furniture, Weingort spent eleven months working with the team at West Village GC renovating the space and bringing everything back down to earth. Naturally, they had their heart set on vintage mid-century furniture, but did not own any collectible pieces at the time. They wanted Weingort to build their collection, and wanted only long-lasting timeless classics they felt familiarity with and could relate to.

Weingort was able to procure a number of standout pieces for her client, including those by Martin Eisler and Carlo Hauner, Pierre Jeanneret, Sergio Rodrigues, Serge Mouille and Geraldo de Barros, mixed with commissions by contemporary artists like Peter Marigold and Tadanori Tozawa, Celine Cannon, Jonathan Nesci and Casey Johnson.

Weingort's work really comes to the fore amid the sea of neutrals, decisive colors and walnut tones in the living and dining area, a self-confessed favourite room.

Photography: portrait by Jessica Kassin, project by Adrian Gaut. Styling: Colin King

Joséphine Fossey

Above all else, it is the desire to prioritise an artistic approach that prevails. While interior architects would generally start by restructuring a space and then move on to decorating their walls with works of art, Joséphine Fossey reverses the process. Before any project, she looks into the history of the premises, breathes in its atmosphere, and considers its future uses in order to define an overall concept. From preliminary sketches through to accessorizing and operational development, her proposals always consider how the client will look at, play around with and adopt the spaces. It is a matter of defining a new way of living that is led by art. In this respect, the designer is reviving precepts dear to the powerful and free-thinking Arts & Crafts movement, whereby art pervades every aspect of daily life. This notion of total art is the founding principle of Joséphine Fossey's approach.

Regarding each programme as unique, she sources and commissions artists who she accompanies throughout the creative process. She always develops spaces that are rooted in their particular context. For the first house of the Iconic House collection, she has entirely redesigned a farmhouse in Les Baux de Provence in the spirit of an artist's house. As strategy consultant, interior architect and art curator, she manages every aspect of the projects.

From her Swedish mother, Joséphine Fossey acquired a sensitivity to Scandinavian design. She developed a taste for simple, uncluttered spaces that emanate a sense of well-being, an intimate and welcoming atmosphere. While she favours the use of natural materials and craftsmanship - natural wood, cut stone, wickerwork - she stirs up her fit-outs with artistic interventions tinged with Surrealism.

From her early days as a specialist in the Impressionist and Modern department of Christie's, Joséphine Fossey has retained a pronounced taste for historical research into the origins, the provenance of works. However, she quickly felt the desire to turn towards a more creative activity. In 2013, she co-founded an agency specialized in curating artworks and styling decorative objects, for private clients and hotel groups alike. She worked on the renovation of the Lutetia Hotel in Paris, on Rosewood Vienna, and on the fit-out of the Seabourn Venture expedition ship. In 2021, feeling the need to reposition her artistic sensibility at the very heart of her work, she founded Joséphine Fossey Office. Accompanied by a team of seven, artistic directors, interior architects, curators and graphic designers, she leads a creative laboratory off the beaten track.

www.josephinefossey.com

Iconic house L'Etoile des Baux, Provence

The first house in the Iconic House collection, L'Etoile des Baux is a farmhouse with a décor designed by Joséphine Fossey.

Located in the Alpilles, L'Etoile des Baux inaugurates a catalog of high-end properties for rent, scattered throughout France.

Thibaud Elzière and Robin Michel, the founders of Iconic House, have entrusted the decoration of their first hotel house to Joséphine Fossey Office.

This Provençal farmhouse built into the rock was transformed into an artist's house by the creative strategy and artistic curation agency. A project built around creative people - both designers and artists - chosen to give another dimension to this unusual place to live.

A fresco by ceramist Florence Bamberger, sculptures by Thalia Dalecky and photos by Romain Laprade decorate the 650 m² space. A warm house, designed for friends and family, which can accommodate up to 16 guests.

Photography: portrait by Noel Manlili, project by Eve Campestrini & Mr Tripper

Maike Borst

Studio &Space was founded by designer Maike Borst. For 9 years she worked at some of Amsterdam's most celebrated design agencies, with an emphasis on retail and interior design. With Studio &Space she loves working on both commercial and high-end residential projects.

Clients of her studio receive both international experience and local, personal attention.

Studio &Space is built on the passion to make this world a more beautiful place. More inspiring, mindful and connected.

They create spaces and experiences that bring to life your dreams and stories. Authentic spaces that connect you with the things you truly care about.

Residential or commercial spaces, temporary or permanent, local or abroad. Maike and her team translate your dreams to a concept that's unique for you; from the bigger picture to the smallest details.

Eindhoven Residence

Maike Borst is proud to reveal the complete renovation of a 1970s residence in a leafy neighbourhood in Eindhoven, The Netherlands for fashion entrepreneur Lotte Drijvers from BYLOTTE. Through the renovation process, an interactive client-designer rapport was established between Maike and Lotte to bring this family home to life.

The design was inspired by the era's mid-century modernism and transformed the residence in a contemporary family home with a touch of glam. The home's exterior was upgraded with a large mahogany wooden carport and front doors, allowing for a welcoming and sheltered entrance. Dormers were added to the upstairs floors to allow for more room and daylight in the kids bed- and playrooms.

Having some awkward partitions, the building's ground floor was stripped back and opened up to the garden in the back, thus creating a large free-flowing kitchen and living area.

The kitchen itself, crafted from warm alder wood with some sweeping curves, focuses around a large island with wooden top, while the wooden folding window reveals an outdoor bar for long summer nights.

The building already featured a sunken lounge area, which was transformed into a conversation pit with an inviting 10-meter long custom sofa. For even more warmth and coziness, a lowered ceiling was created from alder wooden panels in a multi-directional geometric pattern.

Shag carpeting, rich upholstery and brushed copper fixtures lend the upstairs rooms a warm and luxurious feel, while the plastered walls and soft curves are being continued. Both master and kids bathrooms feature Ceppo di Gre tiling and custom wooden cabinetry to expand on the 1970s aesthetics.

Construction management: Bouwaccount. Interior builder: Verschuren Interieurbouw / 't Maathuys. Lighting: Lightboxx.

Photography: Thibault De Schepper

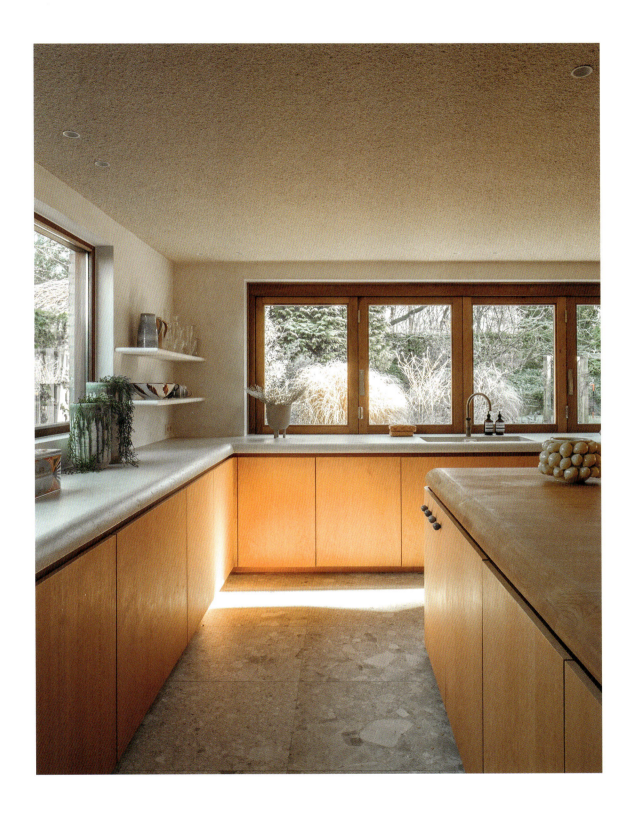

Stef Claes

Architect Stef Claes designs timeless interiors and homes with rich simplicity, earthy tones and interesting perspectives. By constantly blending interior and architecture, he focuses on the experience and developed a powerful design language of his own.

Stef Claes lives in Geneva but has been realising projects all over Europe since 2014. From an early age, he wanted to be an architect - inspired by the houses around him and always busy sketching ground plans and homes.

Stef studied Architecture at the Sint Lucas in Ghent and afterwards travelled around the world to continue his studies, do internships and gain experience. His studies led him to Lisbon and Madrid, he worked for some time in Los Angeles at the agency that ran the John Lautner Foundation, he was apprenticed in Paris to none other than the Japanese master Shigeru Ban who is known from the Centre Pompidou-Metz and in Malaysia he worked on some hotel projects of the Aman Group. So the interior designer has a lot of international experience and a great passion for his profession and you can see that in his projects.

In his designs, Claes always combines interior with architecture. This way he comes to his own personal architectural language because the designer doesn't try to pursue a certain style and just tries to do his own thing and be himself. "The human side of a design makes all the difference," he says. With simple but powerful colours and materials, Claes always creates timeless designs that are warm, rich, subdued and earthy. His many travels and other cultures are a great inspiration for his work, as is mid-century Modernism.

www.stefclaes.com

North Sea Residence

Stef Claes created this residence in the exclusive seaside resort Knokke (Belgian coast) as a vacation home for expats coming back to Belgium from Singapore.

The interior has unmistakable Southeast Asian influences - the clients and Stef Claes had worked together before, and a trusting relationship had developed between them.

In this family weekend home, contemporary and vintage furniture are harmoniously blended. The interior is refined and subtle but not too chic, rather understated - not too monumental, but very warm and livable, convivial too.

The fireplace takes center stage, like a totem, which meant that the architect and developer's plan had to be completely modified. It is a kind of "no man's land" in the middle that creates a luxurious sense of space. The bench was the first piece of furniture chosen - long before the first sketch was made. The bedrooms with high baseboards in Bahamas style add another vacation feel.

Photography: Eric Petschek

Guillaume Gibert
and Baptiste Rischmann

Interior designers Guillaume Gibert and Baptiste Rischmann created their agency RMGB in 2011 after completing their studies at the Institut Supérieur des arts appliqués (Lisaa) and the Ecole nationale supérieure des arts décoratifs (Ensad), respectively. Their radius of action is mainly limited to the Paris region.

RMGB is very sensitive to artisanal craftsmanship, with the designers playing with a choice of materials that demonstrates above all a contemporary style.

The duo renovated a 1930s house in Saint-Léger-en-Yvelines in an authentic manner, respecting the past. They also designed the new offices for LeCab (17th arrondissement), the Parisian antenna of Espaces Atypiques on boulevard Saint-Germain and the renovation of a 1970s architect's house in Burgundy.

www.rmgb.fr

Renovation of a 1940s villa

Guillaume Gibert and Baptiste Rischmann, founders of RMGB, have authentically restored this 1940s villa in Lambersart (near northern France's Lille). The architectural elements and some well-chosen vintage pieces create an engaging dialogue full of modernity.

When renovating, Guillaume and Baptiste went back to the essence of the villa: superfluous moulures, false beams, etc. were removed and made way for a lighter, more harmonious whole. The modern parquet floor was replaced with a solid carpet in the style of the house when it was built.

In the master bedroom, the original furniture was put back and the floor patterns were reinterpreted in mosaic with an identical color scheme as in the old bathrooms.

In terms of furniture choice and decoration, too, RMGB sought a new sense of meaning while also emphasizing the villa's familial, inviting character. The preference was for characterful, remarkable pieces, without therefore being iconic ... a repertory of mostly finds from flee and antique markets from the 1960s to 1980s, without being too flashy ... For example, the "Boomerang" armchair by Rodolfo Bonetto, the side tables by Gio Ponti, the "chauffeuses" by Bernard Gauvin, ... a chic yet informal interior, open and inviting.

The living room, for example, has a very "playground," feel, everything is modular, nothing is stiff in this home ...

Photography: Matthieu Salvaing

Lotte and Dennis Bruns

DAB Studio is an Amsterdam based interior design studio founded by Lotte and Dennis Bruns, working locally and abroad. They cultivate their projects and support their clients in a way that is unique, personal, and deeply considered. Their process stands out amongst peers with tactility, artistry, and collaboration. With a constant dialogue through every stage from concept to production, DAB's clients feel involved, mentored, and even welcomed in as family.

Together with their team of architects and interior designers, Lotte and Dennis create tailored concepts and designs for projects ranging from private residences to hospitality and commercial projects.

Their work is decidedly contemporary with mid-century and modern influences. The results are elegant, luxurious, richly textured, and timeless interiors.

www.dabstudio.nl

Family Home, Zwaag

Commissioned by clients to transform a family home into a modern place of escapism, DAB Studio created a calm yet soulful interior, inspired by the themes of reflection and forcibility. To create a modern environment of timeless sophistication, which is reflective of the owners' diverging taste in design, while also remaining suitable for the everyday life of a family with three children.

Per client's request, the feminine and masculine vision of their new home are balanced in one curated space. This creates unique areas in line with the client's habits and interests, while imbuing the space with a sense of spaciousness and lightness. A continuity of framed views across the space, created by thoughtful placement of artistic elements, followed by dynamic arrangement of planes, which harmoniously complete the space.

In order to merge all elements of the design, it felt important to prioritize the theme of consistency. The wood of the floor is repeated on the ceiling, whereas the wood used for cabinetry, is continued into the walls of the room. The floor was designed in an unusual pattern, where the planks are laid directly next to each other, aligning its beginning and end. The verticality of the quarter sawn cabinetry, adds a playful and dynamic feel to the space. On the contrary, the hand scraped smoked oak panelling on the floor and the ceiling enhances horizontality, equally to the dark space between the cabinets and the ceiling, thus creating more depth and breathing room.

This creates a well-balanced base for the space, while still keeping in line with the family's desire of creating a spotlight for the central piece, the kitchen island. A focal point, an Arebescato Orobico marble kitchen island, designed with soft edges, conjuring hints of theatre and everyday social activities. Extending its beauty to the countertop surface, as well as the dining room table, creating a real showstopper effect, and consistency with the design.

Extending across the adjacent open-plan kitchen and moving into an informal dining area, we are welcomed by the subtle natural light coming through the window, which is softly reflected on the ceiling. The dining nook is where the family can spend time together, welcome new conversations, and create core memories. The asymmetrical built-in banquette seating feels inviting with its round edges, and adds a dynamic feel to the space.

The linear and circular shapes, just as the dark and bright colours, set the tone for the design of the entire space, from the series of straight and irregular planes enhanced by the deep colour palette, to the contemporary volumes and soft edges creating a harmonious bridge between the two.

The selection of furniture, lighting and art, including the bespoke piece of Frank Gehry's Wiggle Chair. A sculptural reflective dining table paired with a built-in banquette seating, surrounded by art pieces, which add colour, contrast, and texture with its fabric, creating a perfect compromise of elegance and warmth. It is the attention to details which makes the space come together, with an airy but imbued in warmth atmosphere, courtesy of an earthy palette of neutral and tan hues, paired with splashes of green and blue.

Photography: Daniëlle Siobhán

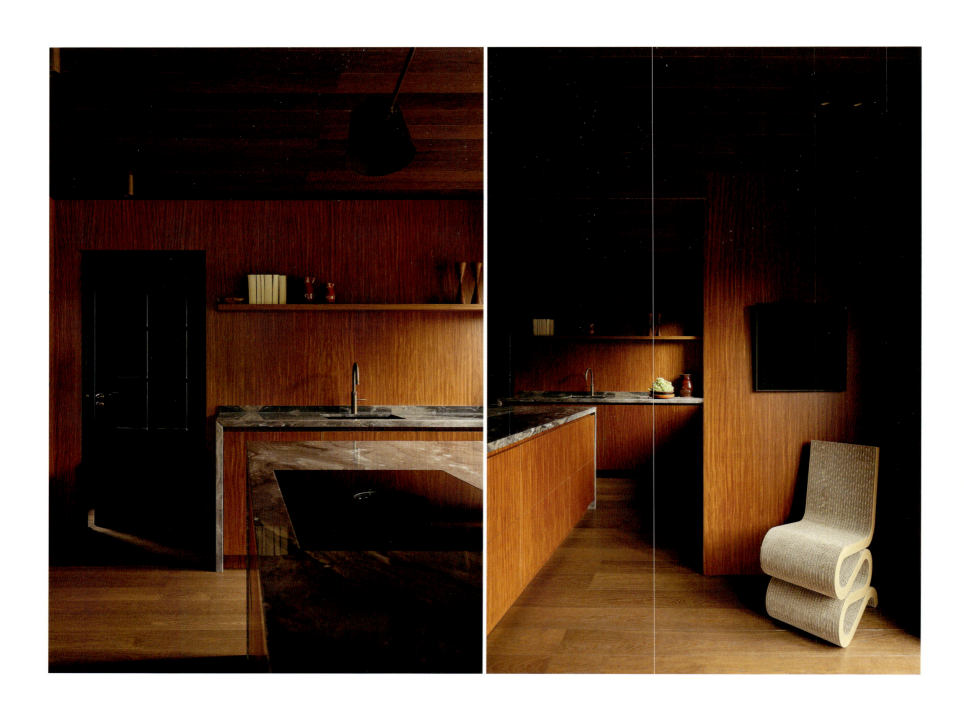

Emily Brown

Emily Lauren Interiors is a design studio rooted in mindful living. They create inviting, intentional spaces with a thoughtful design approach for clients who value a sense of place. Inspired by their northern roots, they embrace the honesty of natural materials that tell a story and age even more beautifully over time. Their humanistic ethos guides their ability to improve the experiences of everyday life through conscious design.

Originally from Canada and raised by a family who respects creativity and craft, Emily studied fine art throughout her childhood and university. After graduating with a BFA in Studio Art, she began her design career as a user experience designer at a major record label in New York City. Upon relocating to Austin, Emily decided to expand her knowledge in design. She returned to school to receive an additional degree in interior design and horticulture while simultaneously opening her design studio.

Emily Lauren Interiors opened in 2018 and continues to create timeless, sustainable designs for residential and commercial spaces.

www.emilylaureninteriors.com

Toro Canyon, Austin (Texas)

Emily and her team began working on Toro Canyon, a large-scale renovation project in the Westlake neighborhood of Austin, TX in 2013.

Due to the scope, the transformation from a dated Texas house to a modern, Scandinavian-inspired home was divided into multiple phases. Metallic wallpaper lined the coffered ceilings and was removed along with copious amounts of Texas limestone from the walls and archways. Drywall was smoothed, 90's style archways were squared off, and white oak flooring was installed throughout the home.

Rather than demolishing the fireplace, the team expanded on the original footprint and connected the chimney breast to the substantial ceilings, creating a grounding feeling in an otherwise oversized room. The fireplace was then plastered in American Clay and the existing herringbone firebricks were painted black, creating a dramatic focal point that comes into awareness immediately upon entering the space. To curate a cozy and welcoming atmosphere in such a grand room, Emily split the space into three activity zones: a quiet library, a social bar, and a conversational living room between the two.

Materials were repeated throughout the entire home to ensure each area feels connected while simultaneously allowing for more intimate experiences. The modern yet timeless look works in perfect harmony with the new homeowners' lifestyle and aesthetic.

Construction: Hudson Builders.

Photography: portrait by Feather & Twine, project by Madeline Harper Photography

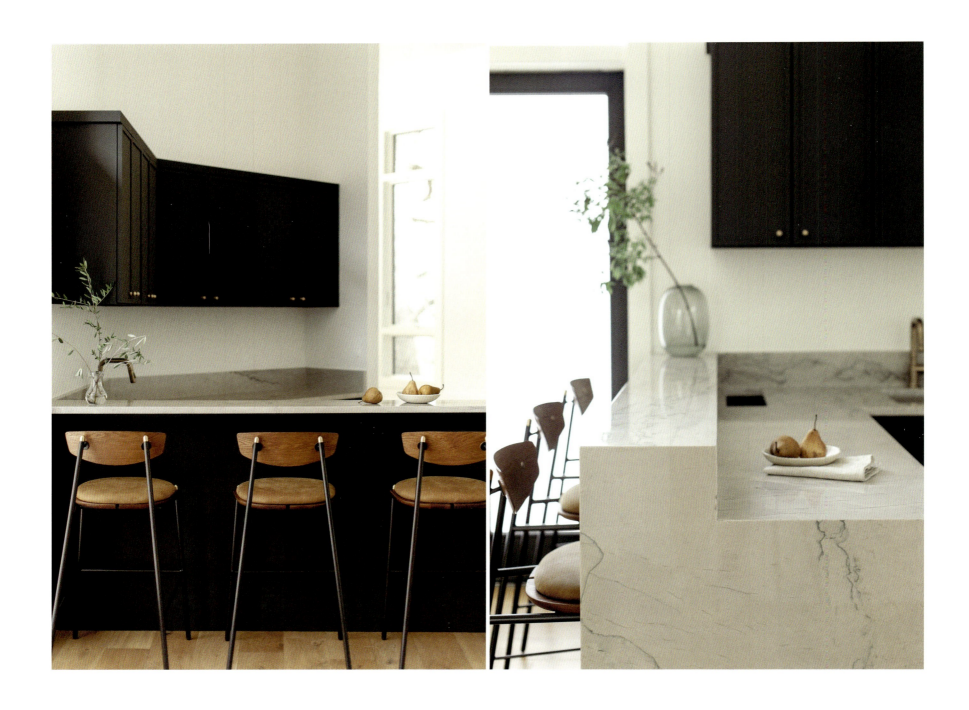

Nathalie Van Reeth

Nathalie Van Reeth studied interior architecture at the Royal Academy of Arts in Antwerp. Her work is inspired by the perfection and refinement of form and function through custom-made creations that exude harmony, intimacy and warmth.

Her vision on interior architecture is based on a few strong power lines: modern and minimal, rough and yet warm, restful and serene, monochrome and with a preponderant sense of space, perspective and light. Her work radiates a certain serenity.

Nathalie loves the austerity, her projects have a sacral power, yet have also been conceived with a human sensibility, with a lot of attention to light, color, texture and natural materials.

She has a penchant for monochromatic spaces with a particular focus on contemporary art.

For Nathalie, minimalism is a result of the essence of things: searching for purity, simple beauty, the presence of timeless spaces, the use of noble, honest and natural materials, and the perpetual quest for perfection.

Always putting things into perspective, no nonsense, and at the same time with a strong sense of harmony, refinement and stillness in an interior.

Nature plays a dominant part in her vision: in all Nathalie's designs the outside environment is in harmony with the client's living environment.

This illustrates, in a very individual sense, how much attention Van Reeth pays to the proper choice of materials, perfect proportions, and the urge for perfection in form and function.

She is very pragmatic in this: no "l'art pour l'art" but always creations made to measure for the client, beautiful, harmonious, sober and refined, but also user-friendly, intimate and radiating warmth.

A lived-in look but in a sober design.

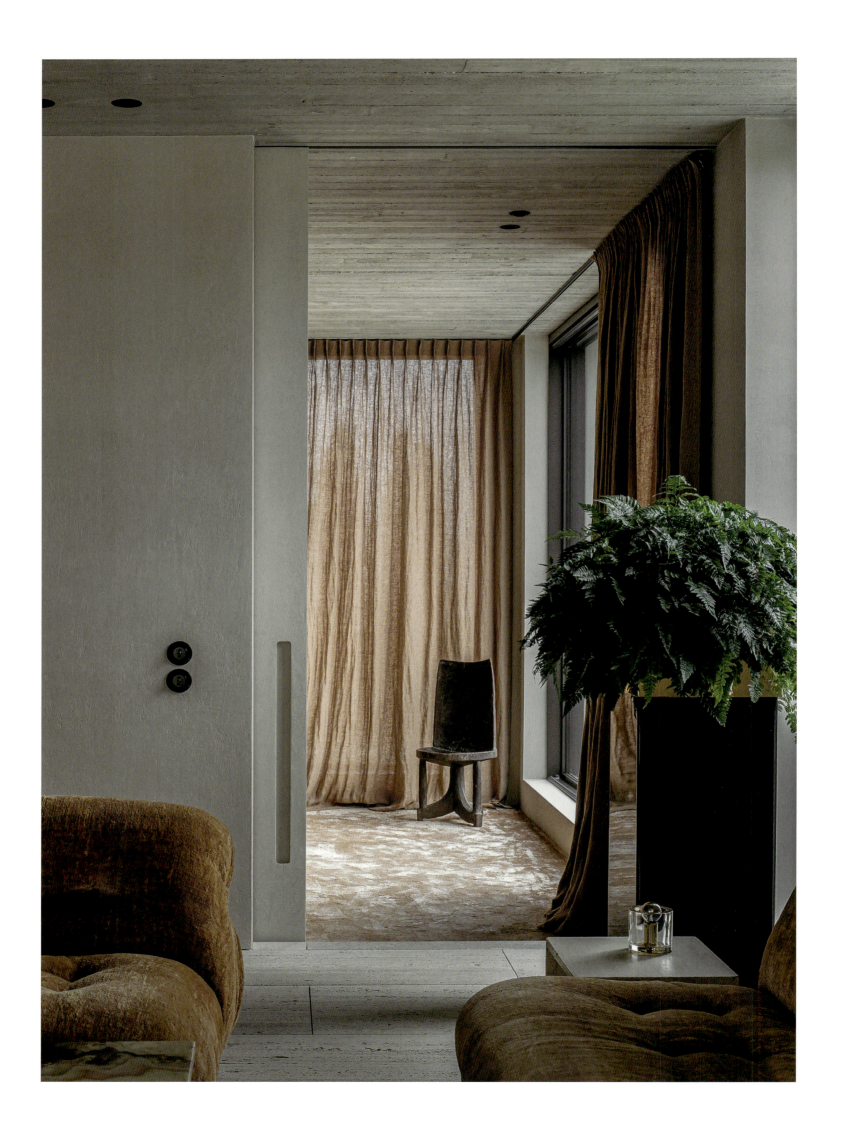

Penthouse MB

This magnificent penthouse is located on the edge of a park, flanked by terraces all around, nestling in the height of the trees.

150 square meter (or approximately 1620 square foot), the idea was the nonchalance of a loft, to evolve freely in the space and having the feeling of living in a hotel.

A choice of materials ranging from gray travertine, through solid walnut, and raw concrete, and a touch of sensuality with a smooth carpet for the bedroom and the bathroom ...

The customers being aesthetes and fine collectors of beautiful vintage furniture, this project by Nathalie Van Reeth has a lived-in, sensual, warm and serene character.

Photography: Cafeine (Thomas De Bruyne). Portrait by Alexander D'Hiet

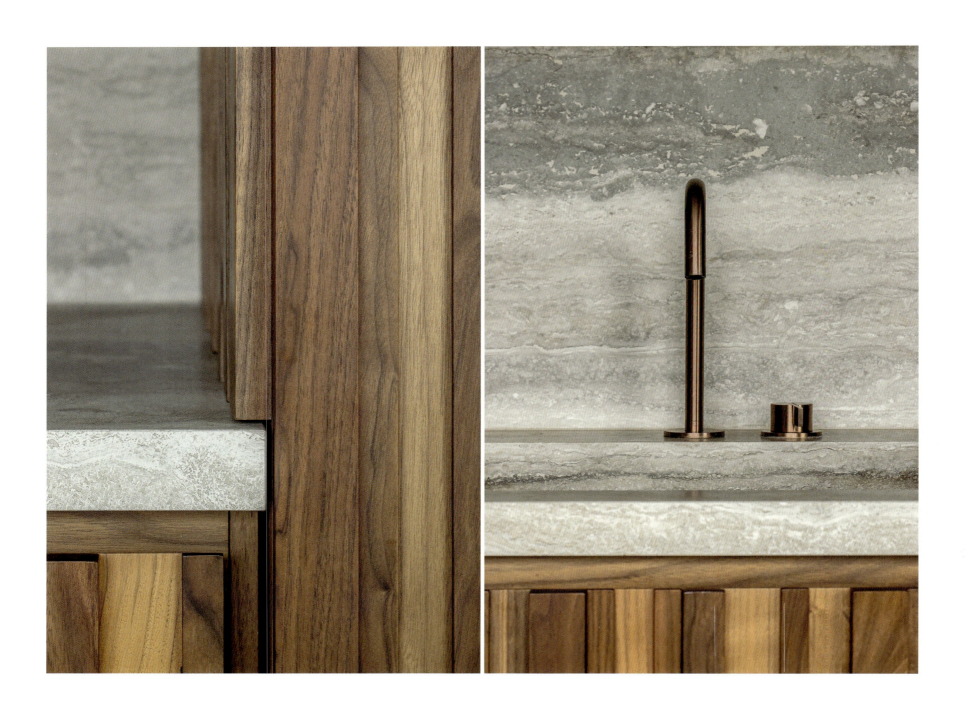

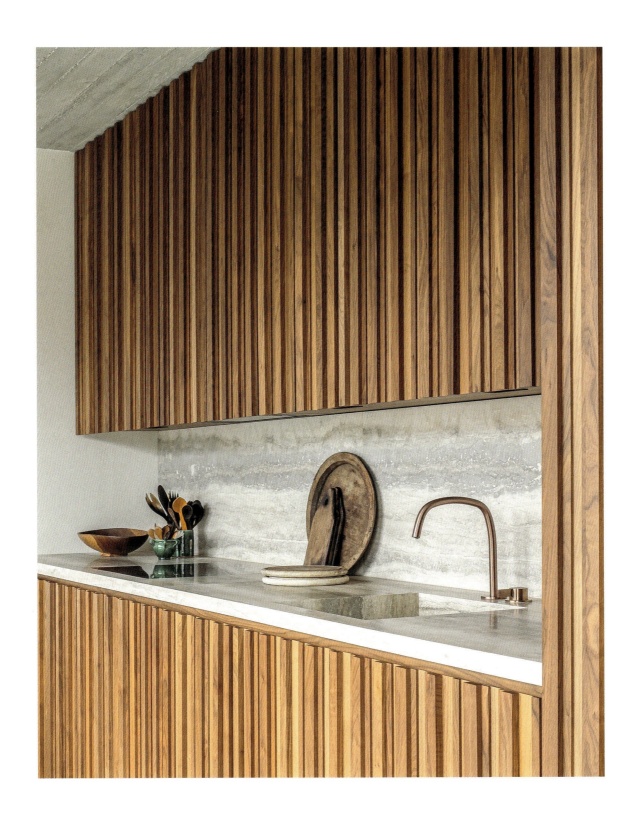

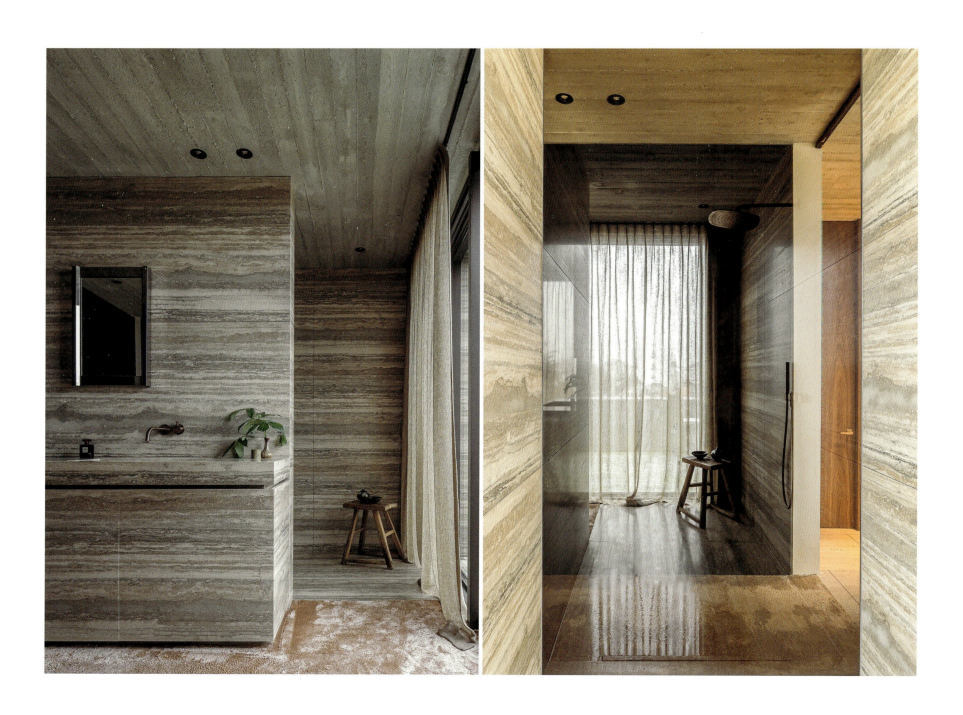

Anne Derasse

Of Belgian origin, Anne Derasse shares her life between Belgium and France, from her two historic residences which she has restored, the Ancienne Nonciature in Brussels and the Château de Montmoreau in Charente, a listed Historic Monument from the 12th and 15th centuries. Interior designer, she holds a master's degree and an aggregation in Art History from the University of Brussels.

Her journey leads her to prestigious projects: boutiques, museums, restaurants, images of luxury brands, castles, to focus on the art of living, both in contemporary and historical settings.

Through her intimacy with the past, which also encompasses its emotional aura, Anne sees restoration with an approach that reconciles rigorous knowledge and artistic sensitivity, without ever forgetting the trace, sign of the passage of time.

Her approach is a synthesis of interior architecture, art and heritage. She creates her projects as a whole, like a "Gesamtkunstwerk", and gives birth to timeless universes, combining the history of places and contemporary creation.

Anne's style is timeless, elegant and warm, far from ephemeral fashions. From interior design to the choice of artworks, her projects have been the subject of numerous publications and a monograph.

www.annederasse.be

Ancienne Nonciature - Brussels

The project presented is the back house of the Ancienne Nonciature, showroom and offices of Anne Derasse in Brussels.

The front house is a mansion, which was the Vatican embassy in the 19th century, of which the chapel remains, where Anne has reinterpreted the decor that had disappeared, like a precious jewel crowned with its celestial vault.

The back house was a squalid garage, she turned it into an elegant loft facing the garden that separates the two houses.

To enhance her pure architectural lines and create her hushed atmospheres, Anne works with light, paradoxically through dark and subtle tones. Sophisticated materials are then revealed with nuance and mystery, between light and shadow.

In search of a total symbiosis, Anne designs all the integrated furniture and creates the mobile furniture. With attention to proportions and the smallest details, they are thought more like volumes where the sobriety of their geometry receives luxurious coverings, thus generating visual and tactile emotion. The exceptional fabrics, the braided leathers and suedes, are chosen from the best manufacturers and creators of renowned textiles and implemented by craftsmen, perpetuating traditional know-how. Anne also advises her clients on the choice of artworks and the development of their collection. In her places of residence and work, she lives surrounded by her personal collection and the works of her companion Jörg Bräuer, artist and photographer.

Photography: Jörg Bräuer

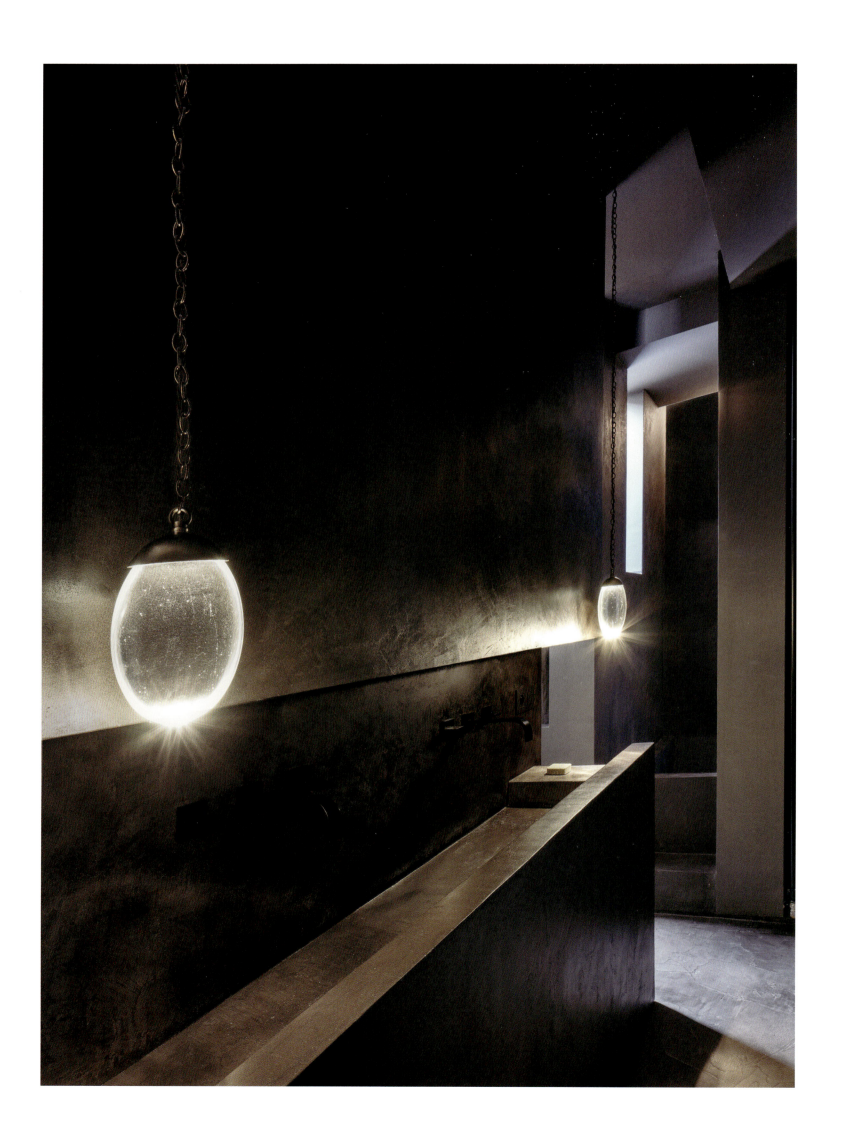

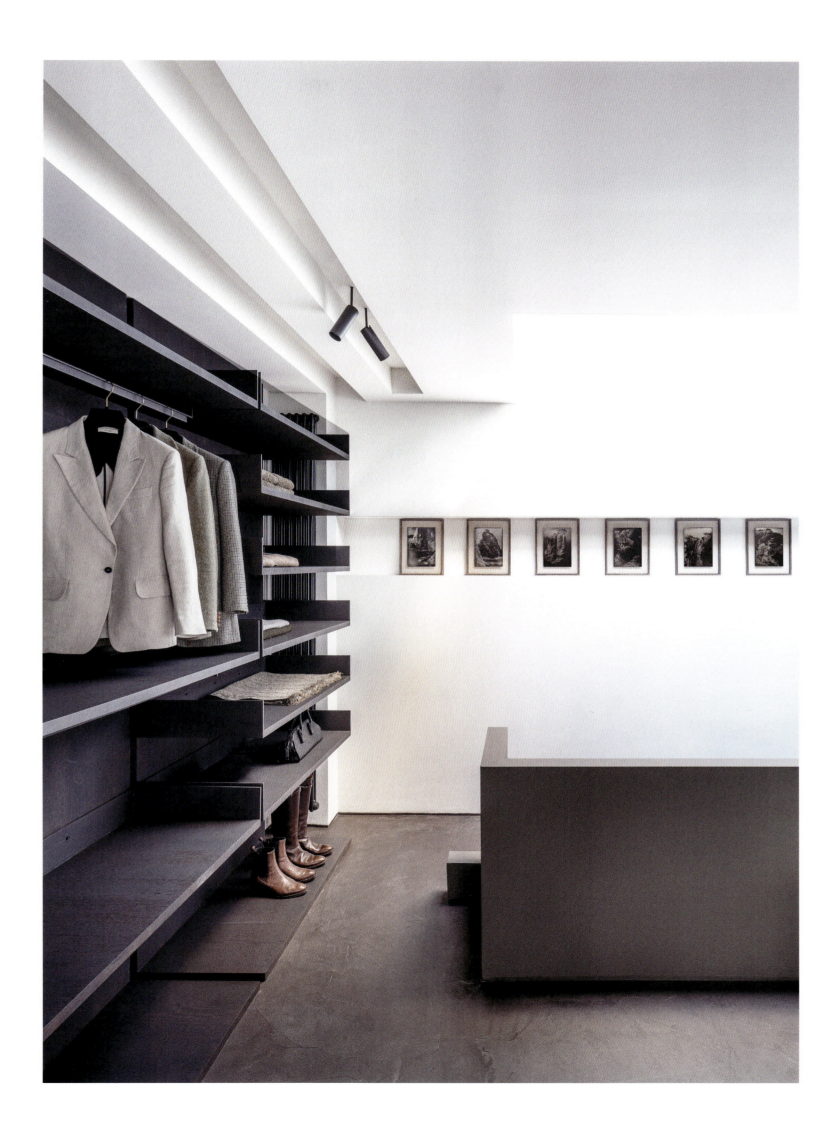

Bicci de' Medici

The creative vision behind Belgian brand Bicci de' Medici, shaped by Sander Motmans, stems from a deep-seated emotion and an unwavering passion for craftsmanship. Growing up surrounded by inspiration, his grandfather's work as an engineer for Philips and the beautiful settings with flower bouquets created by his mother, combined with his father's entrepreneurial spirit, all contributed to Sander's drive to pursue a career in design. This led him to make the pivotal decision at fifteen years old to switch from science and mathematics to architecture and art college.

After obtaining a master's degree in graphic design, Sander felt the need to master the three-dimensional aspect more, so he continued his university studies and earned another master's degree in Liberal Arts. The graduation exhibition allowed him to create a large architectural installation that included self-designed furniture, vases, sculptures, paintings, and limited-edition garments, which inspired Sander to continue his creative journey.

In 2014, during his studies, Sander founded his design studio and initially focused on graphic work and renders for himself. He soon began working as an interior and exterior architect, where he became increasingly familiar with the collections of established brands. However, despite the vast range of options available, he couldn't help but feel that some essential, timeless pieces were missing. Sander started imagining, drawing, and producing pieces on his own. This laid the foundation for Bicci de' Medici as he sought to fill the gap in the market with his designs. Gradually this became a small collection and Sander was asked by other (interior) architects and stores if they could use the pieces in their projects and showrooms. That note set the ball rolling…

Today, Bicci de' Medici stands for classic beauty and durability, with a focus on handcrafted, unique design pieces that are the result of Sander's passion for craftsmanship and his lifelong pursuit of visually appealing aesthetics and creativity.

Named after the light limestone, Pietra di Medici, used for one of its initial creations in 2018, and as a tribute to the influential Giovanni di Bicci of the Florentine de' Medici family, Bicci de' Medici embodies a classic beauty and durability, inspired by a passion for ultimate craftsmanship and a love for natural materials. They prioritize avoiding overproduction, which is achieved through gaining a deeper understanding of their clients' needs, wants, and lifestyles. During the design process, they offer some standard sizes, but they are willing to tailor practically every piece. Working closely with architects, interior designers, and clients, to guarantee that each piece is custom-made to fit perfectly in its surroundings. While the studio previously handled most of the production, it now collaborates with specialized partners to bring each piece to fruition. For example, a table may have undergone multiple stages of crafting by various artisans before being meticulously hand-finished to perfection.

Dedicated to preserving its natural aesthetic and unwavering commitment to craftsmanship, Bicci de' Medici proudly collaborates with like-minded parties to bring its vision to life, while striving to remain socially responsible and true to its roots.

www.biccidemedici.com

The beauty of imperfection

Bicci de' Medici is a brand renowned for its commitment to using sustainable and natural materials. The choice to use solid, responsible, and natural materials was an obvious one, as they are committed to providing timeless pieces that can last for generations. Today, with the increasing importance of environmental responsibility, it is imperative that production methods are not heavily taxing and that the materials and products used are not inferior. In addition to the use of sustainable materials, Bicci de' Medici also appreciates the natural imperfections that develop on these materials over time, such as the patina that forms on natural stone after a few years. The brand encourages people to embrace and cherish these imperfections, as they tell a story, carry a history, and are a reminder of the passage of time. As a result, certain pieces from the Bicci de' Medici collection are deliberately made imperfect, reflecting the transience of life and the unique beauty that can only be achieved through natural processes. The brand also values the use of materials such as wool, linen, clay, wood, and natural stone, which already have natural imperfections, further adding to the story and history of each piece. The imperfections in these materials are seen as a testament to their authenticity and the journey they have taken. By incorporating these elements into their designs, Bicci de' Medici is able to create pieces that are not only aesthetically pleasing but also meaningful, reflecting the brand's commitment to responsible and sustainable practices.

The Belgian design studio is known not only for its own collection but also for its unique collection of «objets trouvés». Over the years, they have collected furniture and other vintage decoration pieces by some of the most iconic designers, such as Jean Prouvé, Charlotte Perriand, Pierre Jeanneret, Le Corbusier, Isamu Noguchi, Pierre Chapo, and others. The blend of old and new pieces gives the interiors a soulful, individualistic dimension. When they work on a residential interior project, the founder is dedicated to incorporating lived-in, authentic pieces into his designs, and if possible, even incorporating pieces that have been cherished by the client for generations, to create truly one-of-a-kind and personalized spaces.

Sander encompasses a natural and bespoke approach to design but he does not limit himself to a specific style. He aspires towards a neutral, universally appealing aesthetic that draws inspiration from his Belgian/Flemish background. Being situated in the capital of Europe, Belgium boasts a rich multicultural society that has exposed Motmans to a multitude of different styles, influencing and inspiring him to create a balanced, sophisticated variant of the "Flemish style." This may also explain why he as a Belgian designer finds Japanese design so appealing, as it embodies a similar restraint and refinement.

The team at Bicci de' Medici embraces simplicity and neutral hues, lending a sense of peace and balance to living spaces. Their designs can be easily incorporated into a range of interiors, whether modern and minimal or classic and ornate.

Bicci de' Medici sets itself apart from other design and interior design studios in both its offerings and approach. As a small company, they have the flexibility to embrace new ideas and challenge conventional norms. They don't limit themselves to a strict definition or approach, instead opting for a fluid structure that encourages collaboration and growth. This allows them to work closely with clients, designers, craftsmen, and architects to bring their unique visions to life. Bicci de' Medici also prioritizes collaboration with other design brands and designers, valuing new combinations and innovative ideas. There is no need to reinvent the wheel.

Photography: Studio Waow & Ilse Raps. Portrait by Ilse Raps. Styling: Bicci de' Medici

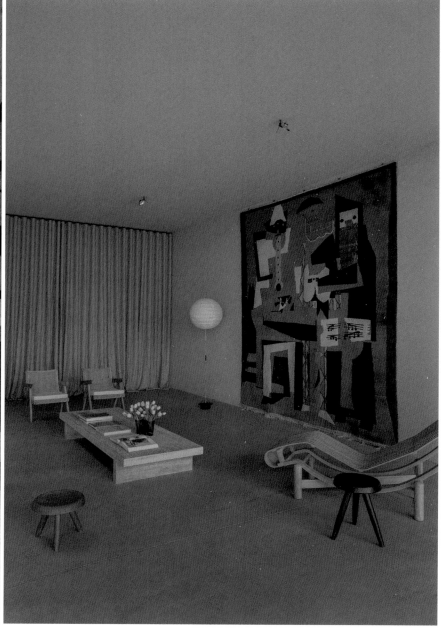

PUBLISHER
BETA-PLUS nv/sa
Avenue Louise 367
B-1050 Brussels
www.betaplus.com

DESIGN
Patrick Pierre

© 2023, BETA-PLUS

All rights reserved.

No part of this publication may be reproduced,
stored in a retrieval system, or transmitted
in any form or by any means.

Printed in Belgium.